Accidentally in Love

USA TODAY BESTSELLING AUTHOR
CLAUDIA BURGOA

Also By Claudia Burgoa

Be sure to sign up for my newsletter where you'll receive news about upcoming releases, sneak previous, and also FREE books from other bestselling authors.

ACCIDENTALLY IN LOVE is also available in Audio

The Baker's Creek Billionaire Brothers Series

Loved You Once

A Moment Like You

Defying Our Forever

Call You Mine

As We Are

Yours to Keep

Paradise Bay Billionaire Brothers

My Favorite Night

Faking The Game

Can't Help Love

Along Came You

My Favorite Mistake

The Way of Us

Meant For Me

Finally Found You

Where We Belong

Heartwood Lake Secret Billionaires

A Place Like You

Dirty Secret Love

Love Unlike Ours

Through It All

Better than Revenge

Fade into us

An Unlikely Story

Hard to love

Against All Odds Series

Wrong Text, Right Love

Didn't Expect You

Love Like Her

Until Next Time, Love

Something Like Love

Accidentally in Love

Forget About Love

Waiting for Love

Decker Family Novels

Unexpected Everlasting:

Suddenly Broken

Suddenly Us

Somehow Everlasting:

Almost Strangers

Strangers in Love

Perfect Everlasting:

Who We Are

Who We Love

Us After You

Covert Affair Duet:

After The Vows

Love After Us

The Downfall of Us:

The End of Me

When Forever Finds Us

Requiem for Love:

Reminders of Her

The Symphony of Us

Impossibly Possible:

The Lies About Forever

The Truth About Love

Second Chance Sinners :

Pieces of Us

Somehow Finding Us

The Spearman Brothers

Maybe Later

Then He Happened

Once Upon a Holiday

Almost Perfect

Luna Harbor

Finally You

Perfectly You

Always You

Truly You

My One

My One Regret

My One Desire

The Everhart Brothers

Fall for Me

Fight for Me

Perfect for Me

Forever with Me

Mile High Billionaires

Finding My Reason

Something Like Hate

Someday, Somehow

Standalones

Chasing Fireflies

Until I Fall

Christmas in Kentbury

Chaotic Love Duet

Begin with You

Back to You

Co-writing

Holiday with You

Home with You

Here with You

All my books are interconnected standalone, except for the duets, but if you want a reading order, I have it here ↪ Reading Order

All rights reserved.

By payment of the required fees, you have been granted the non-exclusive, non-transferable right to access and read the text of this e-book on your personal e-reader.

No part of this text may be reproduced, transmitted, downloaded, distributed, decompiled, reverse engineered, stored into or introduced into any information storage and retrieval system, in any form or by any means, whether electronic, photocopying, mechanical or otherwise known or hereinafter invented, without the expressed written permission of the publisher.

Except by a reviewer who may quote brief passages for review purposes.

This book is a work of fiction. Names, characters, brands, organizations, media, places, events, storylines and incidents are the product of the author's imagination or are used fictitiously.

Any resemblance to any person, living or dead, business establishments, events, locales or any events or occurrences, is purely coincidental.

The author acknowledges the trademarked status and trademark owners of various products, brands, and-or restaurants referenced in this work of fiction, of which have been used without permission. The use of these trademarks is not authorized with or sponsored by the trademark owners.

www.claudiayburgoa.com

Copyright © 2023 by Claudia Burgoa

Cover by: Hang Le

Edited by: Susan Bischoff, Sisters Get Lit.erary Author Services, Virginia T. Carey

Dear Reader,

I write highly emotional romances that include thought provoking subjects. If you would like to see a list of them, please check the link below with more information.

TW Website

Happy Reading,
Claudia

To my maternal side of the family— without your unique experiences some of my books wouldn't have been possible.

When we love, we always strive to become better than we are. When we strive to become better than we are, everything around us becomes better too.

— Paulo Coelho, The Alchemist

Chapter One

Kingston

AND IT'S COME DOWN to WildMatch.

On any normal day, you would find me at my office in a Seattle high-rise, signing contracts, acquiring new products, making decisions like determining where we're branching out. But as of right now, the only important decision I need to make in the moment is: How am I going to burn off this pent-up energy my body has accumulated over the past few days while I've been holed up in the small town of Luna Harbor?

You may be wondering why I'm over a hundred and twenty

miles away from Seattle and the comfort of my own home. Unfortunately, that's top secret. The truth is, I'm not entirely sure what's going on with my sister and Seth Bradley, my brother's best friend. They're either chasing after bad guys or… well, I'm confused because no one is giving me a straight answer. From what I've heard, she's being used as bait along with her presumed husband to lure the bad guys out.

All I know is that, until the high-intelligence security company responsible for our safety says it's safe to return home, I'm confined to this small town near the base of the Olympic Mountains, with no access to my computer or my life.

When I get out of here, I'm going to give Seth Bradley a piece of my mind. He's the man responsible for this clusterfuck. And the man who is putting Teddy, my little sister, in danger. A knot forms in my throat just thinking of what can happen to her, but I promptly push the negative thoughts away.

She's going to be okay. Try to focus on other things, like finding a way to distract yourself.

I glance around the courtyard of the Luna Harbor Inn, my gaze wandering from place to place. The trees and plants have been trimmed impeccably. The cobblestone walkways are lined with white and gray pebbles and rustic lanterns, which create a sense of warmth and comfort during the night. Yesterday, I stayed out here enjoying the tranquil atmosphere until midnight reading a book.

Thankfully, once again there's no one else around. The area is just as peaceful and calming. Not something I usually seek in my daily life, but circumstances call for it. If I weren't sharing the room with my brothers, Myles and Fletcher, I would be upstairs with my own thoughts debating what to do with my day instead of out here.

Fuck, this is not what I expected to be doing this Tuesday morning. I wish I were home. No, better yet, I want to be in my office with my own things. Instead, I'm sitting on a bench in a courtyard, staring at a phone given to me while I'm here for who knows how long. I'm so worked up—I need to do something with this energy right now—I consider the options available to me.

Earlier today, Fletch had the audacity to tell me to relax. Like that's even an option. Actually, that word is outright forbidden from my vocabulary.

Hence, why I'm downloading the WildMatch app. Myles swears it's the best hookup app available on the market. So, why not give it a try since there's nothing else to do? Sex might calm me down.

But is it even worth it to create a profile?

Why not... here goes nothing.

Name... should I add my real name?

Nope, that'd be foolish. Eighty percent of the people who are currently in this town know who I am.

"Welcome to WildMatch." Startled by a female robotic voice, I quickly turn down the volume. "This app was designed just for you. An adventurous person who's looking for short-term, casual encounters and fun. We offer a safe and discreet platform so you can connect with others who share similar desires."

I look around the courtyard, making sure no one heard that.

I wish I had my earbuds with me. Since I don't, and there's no one around, I continue with the tour.

"WildMatch uses a location-based search to show you a potential match. We have built-in safety features to ensure a safe and enjoyable experience. You can use our free plan, but if you subscribe…"

I switch off the tour. I shouldn't be surprised that they're trying to sell me a membership. If I were in Seattle, it would be worth it, but here… I'll be lucky if I find someone who's willing to help me.

The prompt to fill out my details appears again…

Name: *William "Willy" Davis*

Age? I consider disclosing my age, but settle on thirty-five instead of thirty-eight.

About me? I think about who I really am—six feet four with dark brown eyes. They're almost black—like my soul. Dark hair. Athletic build. I'm not a gym buff, but I like to keep myself in shape. I own Earth Fields Market, the fastest-growing organic grocery chain in the world. And I did it on my own merit, not because I'm Donovan St. James's son.

I graduated summa cum laude from Columbia University. People probably think I don't give two fucks about the world. But I do. I'm an environmentalist. I'm the eldest of seven siblings. My brothers and little sister are all I care about.

But then I think, will that get me laid? Probably not. So instead, I go with:

About Me: *I'm a driven and successful entrepreneur who enjoys working hard and playing harder. I love to travel and explore new cultures* and am passionate about staying fit and healthy. In my free time, I enjoy playing tennis, skiing, and golfing.

Interests: *Traveling, fitness, tennis, skiing, golfing, and fine dining.*

Looking for: *I'm not looking for anything too serious right now, but I'm open to exploring new connections and seeing where things go. I'm looking for a woman who is confident, independent, and fun-loving. I'm attracted to women who are intelligent, ambitious, and have a sense of humor.*

Ideal match: *My ideal match is someone who is confident, intelligent, and passionate about her work and interests. She should be able to hold her own in a conversation and be comfortable in any setting. I'm looking for someone who can challenge me intellectually, and who is open to exploring new experiences together.*

If you think we might be a good match, send me a message, and let's see where this goes.

I'm surprised when a notification pops up instantly: Congratulations! You have a new match. I'm not sure about the peaches, water drops, and eggplant emojis popping like confetti on the screen. Do they have to do that? It's kind of... tacky, isn't it?

When I tap the notification, I see a blurred picture and the profile of my match. Sofia Hernandez. She's twenty-five.

I'm a fun-loving and adventurous person who enjoys trying new things and meeting new people. I'm a graphic designer by profession, but I also have a wild side that I like to indulge from time to time. I'm fluent in English and Spanish, and I love to dance to Latin music.

Her interests are traveling, trying new foods, dancing, hiking, playing guitar, and watching romantic comedies.

I'm looking for someone who is confident, adventurous, and open-minded. I'm not interested in a serious relationship right now, but I'm open to exploring new connections and having some fun along the way. I'm attracted to men who are spontaneous, passionate, and who know how to have a good time.

The keywords are there, *not interested in a serious relationship.* That's music to my ears. We could try to work something out for the next few days or weeks. I continue reading as I try to figure out how to contact her.

My ideal match is someone who is spontaneous, adventurous, and knows how to have a good time. He should be confident and comfortable in his own skin and be able to hold his own in a conversation. I'm looking for someone who can keep up with me, and who is open to exploring new experiences together.

If you think we might be a good match, send me a message, and let's see where this goes.

Well, Sofia. I want to see how things can go. I search for how to connect with this perfect woman and how to find a picture of her. Did I upload my picture when I created a profile?

Nope. I'm scrambling to see how to fix my profile and connect with her when a female voice startles me, "You're new at this, aren't you, St. James?"

When I look up, I'm struck by the beauty standing right in front of me. Dark blue soulful eyes that contrast with her olive skin. She has a small turned-up nose and pouty lips that I wouldn't mind kissing. For a second, I want them wrapped around my cock, but the fantasy doesn't last long.

Myka Cantú is beautiful and elegant, and… she's off-limits.

Off-limits.

Her brother and I have been friends since third grade. Just last week I signed a contract with their family brewery. There's no way I'm going to hook up with her.

No way.

But what if... she's not here to talk about WildMatch? I'm sure there's another reason why she's here, right?

"What do you mean by 'new at this'?" I ask in confusion and stare at the bench where I'm sitting. "This is made for sitting, isn't it?"

She releases a soft laugh, then shows me her phone. "Wild-Match." It's just one word, but the implications are astronomical.

I stare at her before saying, "How do you know?"

"The matches are by location, not by interests," she explains. "The moment someone is nearby, it alerts you. There's no special algorithm. Just two horny people who might get lucky... if the circumstances are right."

I frown. "How do you know it's me?"

She shrugs. "When I got the notification, I was in the lobby. You're the only person within a point-zero-one-mile radius from me—with a phone." She points at the artifact in my hand.

"You're Sofia Hernandez?"

She nods. "Yep. That's me, *William.*"

"This isn't what you think," I spit the words. Then narrow my gaze. "And you're not twenty-five."

Myka gives me a challenging look. "So, you didn't try to hook up with someone because you're bored?"

I open my mouth, but I can't say anything. This is little Myka. I've known her since she was four and I was nine. Her oldest brother, Iskander, will probably kill me if he learns that I made a pass at his sister. She might be a gorgeous woman with a striking body, but I have to stay away from her.

Myka laughs. "Cat got your tongue?"

"No. I'm…"

The corner of her lip lifts. "Here's what I think. You downloaded the app, started a profile and hoped to find a quick fuck. But I bet you didn't finish the tour, so you barely know how this works. If you had, you would've been able to see my pictures and maybe tap once to avoid this awkward encounter."

"You're probably right." Probably? She knows exactly what happened. I'm dumbfounded and horny. If there weren't some unwritten rules that I can never have her, I would drag her to my room.

I can't.

I shouldn't.

Myka is off-limits.

Myka equals no sex.

But Myka is so fucking hot.

"Oh, I know I'm right, but I'm not done with my theory. You were expecting to match with some stranger. Instead, little Myka Cantú caught you." She licks her lips. "Fortunately for you, I'm not little anymore."

I'm almost panting at her sultry voice. Who is this woman? And can I break the rules? What if I have just a lick? One fuck, and I swear I'll leave her alone.

No, you can't, St. James.

She looks at her nails and then back at me. "This is such a shame."

"What?"

"Your body wants me, but your mind is fighting the urge to fuck me. That's unfortunate and sad. We're both losing because you have some weird hang-up about having sex with me. That's silly. We're both consenting adults, aren't we?"

I nod, speechless. She's right. This version of Myka is so different from *little Myka*, the one I used to know. She's beautiful, and her strength and confidence make her even more attractive. If I wasn't a one-time guy, I'd drag her home with me and never let go.

I'm taken aback by my sudden thoughts. I always used to prioritize physical attraction, but now Myka has sparked something far deeper in me. I'm so excited, yet terrified all at once—could I really be looking for something more than just a casual fling?

Myka stares at me expectantly.

I straighten my shoulders and say, "I agree. We're two consenting adults."

"Then, follow me," she orders.

"Umm, where?"

"My house." She smirks. "Unless big old Kingston St. James is afraid of little Myka."

"Umm, I'm not afraid of you. Of course not."

"Good, because I don't bite." She chews on her bottom lip seductively. "Only suck, if you ask nicely."

She turns around and begins to walk away. Can I even follow her with this raging hard-on? I'm so turned on by her that I can't think straight. All I want is to be inside Myka Cantú.

Chapter Two

Myka

WHAT THE FUCK are you thinking, Myka?

I'm not sure if I should scold myself for being so bold or throw a big party for scoring a... Did I seriously say all those things to Kingston St. James?

I mean, he's Kingston fucking St. James.

He's one of the most striking and impressive men in Washington State—if not the country.

He's every woman's dream. Rugged and masculine facial features like Jensen Ackles, but with piercing brown eyes and dark hair. With a chiseled jawline, sharp cheekbones, and a well-trimmed beard, he's one hell of a man... and my brother Iskander's oldest friend. Clad in a black t-shirt, his muscular physique is on full display, revealing broad shoulders, bulging biceps, and perhaps even a six- or eight-pack abdomen.

He exudes confidence, strength, and sex appeal.

Kingston St. James was too old and out of my league while growing up. Now... well, he's just not my type.

I prefer subtle men who don't seek attention and blend among us mortals.

Kingston is like a god—a mix between Zeus and Hades. He embodies the powers and domains of the king of the gods and the lord of the underworld. He's respected by mortals and immortals.

Does he fiercely protect his territory and those who belong to him?

Is he a god in bed?

Push away the lust and pray that he's not following you. This is a bad idea, Myk.

It's all my fault, you know, because curiosity killed the cat and all that shit. In this case, I'm the cat and might soon die of embarrassment. I have a profile and like to snoop around to see which guys come to Luna Harbor to hook up. But I never use it. Never.

Who knew Kingston St. James would be waiting to hook up with Sofia Hernandez?

"How far is your house?" he asks, his deep baritone voice carrying over the crispy air.

I wave a hand dismissively. "Not far, but I think you should stay. It's for the best."

Inside, my roiling stomach churns in knots. He's not actually interested in me, is he?

Sure, if he were anyone else, I wouldn't mind dragging him to my bedroom, tying him up, and having my wicked way with him. But…

It's been two years since the last time I had sex. And just because someone shows a passing interest in me, doesn't mean I should jump into bed with them… right?

I take a deep breath and plaster on a sarcastic smirk. "If you want to decline the invitation—"

"Oh no," he interrupts me quickly. "I'm definitely interested. Luna Harbor might be magical, but it's suffocating."

I shoot him a judgmental look. "My town isn't suffocating. You're just some big-city mogul, thinking he can get everything he desires right outside his door." We've made it to my house now, and are my palms actually sweaty?

"You got that wrong," he interjects. "If I had my laptop and access to my email, I'd be tucked in my room taking care of myself," he says as we arrive at my doorstep.

I push the handle open and glance at him. "So, are you telling me that all you need is porn and your hand?"

"Ugh, that's not what I meant." He chokes back a laugh, his cheeks flushing.

"Sure… Let's go with that." I quirk an eyebrow, daring him to argue.

He shakes his head in embarrassment. "Listen, this isn't something I often do."

Crossing my arms, I study him with an amused expression. "Why do people feel the need to justify their sex lives?"

He blinks at me, visibly confused.

"You don't have to rationalize your behavior," I explain with a shrug. "As long as you have sex with a consenting adult, no one should give two fucks about your private life."

He gives me a wry smile as I push the door open. "Do you have any filters?"

Chuckling, I shake my head. "Nope. I don't have the time or patience to sugarcoat things for anyone. And maybe this is a bad idea," I caution him as we step inside.

He furrows his brows, looking perplexed. "Why would it be a bad idea? You said it earlier, 'We're two consenting adults.'"

"What if you confuse casual sex and get hung up on me?" I wink at him.

Kingston points at himself. "Me?" He laughs. "Nope. I'm the king of one-night stands."

"No pun intended," I chuckle.

"What about you?"

"I don't do this often," I say. It sounds a lot better than "I don't believe in hookups," and I only have sex with someone I trust.

I raise an eyebrow skeptically as I consider my options. Do I trust Kingston St. James? I decide to go with my gut and take a leap of faith, offering up an idea.

"What if we take on different personas?" I suggest casually, nonchalant as ever. "Me as Sofia Hernandez and you as William... What's the last name you were using?"

He grins mischievously, his gaze sparkling. "It doesn't

matter." He pulls me close, our faces just a breath away. "William and Sofia are gonna have some fun today," he whispers, "and tomorrow, we won't even remember each other's names."

As he pulls me close, I feel my heart racing with anticipation. His body feels strong and secure against mine, and I revel in the warmth of his embrace. With his mouth so near, I feel a tension building, a desire to lean in closer and feel his lips against mine.

I smirk, shaking my head slightly. "So you're unforgettable, huh?"

"Oh, baby." He smirks. "You'll remember I was inside you for days."

Joy swells in my heart and my entire body quivers with anticipation. I want nothing more than to be in his arms, to feel his strength and security wrapping around me, to let him be my safe harbor.

He leans in, and his lips are sweet with the promise of adventure. A spark of electricity passes between us as we kiss. The moment is utter bliss.

"Let's focus on just the now," he whispers against my lips.

But will this one time be enough?

Chapter Three

Kingston

I KISS HER AGAIN, deeper, and suddenly I feel her surrender to me, each movement of her body sending a thrill of excitement through me. My body is alive with a desire I never thought I could feel, and I have the urge to possess her.

To make her mine.

To give her all that I have, and to be one with her in this moment.

My heart races with an intensity that I can't explain.

This kiss ignites a flame within me, a flame that burns with passion. My body is alive with longing, and my heart is filled with the certainty that I have found my true love.

The world around us fades away, and all that exists is her and me. I breathe her in, wanting to feel her warmth against my skin, and lose myself in the depth of her soul.

Right now, at this moment, nothing matters but her. The way she kisses, her touch, and her scent intoxicates me. She smells of gardenias mixed with a hint of jasmine, and it's a scent that matches her beauty and grace.

But, I think, *tonight might not be enough with this woman.*

Don't go there. This is one time only. One night.

"Where's your room?" I ask, already scanning the living room.

She tilts her head and begins to walk away from me. I follow right behind.

"This is a big room," I say, studying the whole place. "Is that your artwork?"

"I don't think I brought you here to take a tour of my house," she says.

When I turn around, I'm struck by her beauty. We just stand for a moment, neither of us saying a word. I can feel my heart skipping a beat as I take a step toward her. Slowly, I reach out and take her hands in mine.

"Are you sure about this?" I ask, my voice trembling slightly.

Myka looks up at me and nods, her eyes burning with intensity. "Yes," she whispers.

I can barely contain my excitement as I move closer to her, our bodies almost touching. Reaching out, I slowly begin to unbutton her sweater, my fingers lightly brushing her skin. She draws in a sharp breath, her eyes closing as I work my way down.

I feel my own breathing accelerate as I push the fabric off her shoulders and let it fall to the floor. She stands before me in just her jeans with her naked breasts on display.

I reach out and brush my thumb over her lips, my touch making her shiver. I can feel the heat radiating from her as I trail my hands south past her collarbone, between the valley of her breasts down to her jeans and begin to unbuckle her belt. She gasps as I slide the zipper down, my fingers lightly caressing her skin as I pull the fabric apart.

For a moment, I pause, mesmerized by the sight of her. She looks like a goddess, her curves accentuated by the faint light coming through the window. I reach for the hem of my shirt and pull it over my head, my pulse quickening with anticipation. With my shirt off, I reach out and slide my hands around her waist, pulling her close to me.

With her skin pressed against mine, our hearts beating in time, we remain still on the cusp of a life-altering moment. Finally, I take a step back and start to remove the rest of my clothing. Her gaze is on me as I unbutton my pants and I step out of them and kick it aside. I stand there in just my boxers, my body trembling with anticipation. I can feel her eyes roaming over my body, taking in every inch of my exposed skin.

I yank her closer and plant a kiss on her lips. She tastes like wild berries picked fresh from the forest. A thrill courses through me as I thoroughly explore her body. My fingers dance across her curves, and she lets out a giggle.

I grasp the nape of her neck and kiss her deeply. Our kiss is electric, our tongues tangling and dancing together. She exhales heavily when I pull away from the kiss, as we watch my fingers drift down her torso, then lower until I reach her inner thigh.

"Are you ready for this?"

She gazes into my eyes, a determined glint in her own. "Yes," she replies firmly. "I want you to touch me… to enjoy me… to take me."

Her fingers lightly dance across the tattoos on my chest as she talks, and my stomach flips. "If you're good," she says with an impish grin, "I'll design your next tattoo."

"And I might let you"—I clear my throat—"but right now, I just want to focus on you." I get down to my knees, pressing a gentle kiss onto her panties before removing them, then exploring her sensitive core with my hand.

She lets out a breathy gasp.

"You're soaking wet, darling. Is this for me?" I murmur against her lips with a smirk, pressing lightly around her heat with my thumb.

"Yes," she whines, pushing herself harder up against me, "just stop teasing me already and show me what you got."

"Lie on the bed."

Myka does as I say without hesitation, her curls fanned against the pillows like a Renaissance painting. She looks like a goddess lying there before me, and my heart swells at her beauty.

I crawl onto the bed before crushing my lips to hers. Myka hisses against my mouth as my thumb circles her heat, teasing her with light touches.

"Are you going to let me eat you? Devour you?" I murmur against her lips as I pull away slightly.

Myka presses herself even closer to me before whispering a single word, "Yes."

I slide my hand across her light-bronze skin as if it were silk, taking in every inch of her body before feeling a gentle tug on the waistband of my boxers—Myka's hand quickly outlining the length of my hard cock beneath the fabric. My breath hitches and my eyes flutter closed as she rubs it gently between her delicate fingers.

Taking a deep breath, I open my eyes and summon up all of my control. "Let's get creative," I suggest with a devious grin before shifting further onto the bed so that I am looming above her.

I slowly trace my finger around her wet pussy and make her moan in response. "Two can play this game, darling."

"King," she pants, her center squeezing around my finger and yearning for more. But before she can get any more of me, I move my hand away from her heat and delicately place it on her soft belly.

She lifts her face and nibbles on my jawline, sending shivers down my spine. I kiss each of her eyelids with tenderness, each of her cheeks with appreciation, and her lips with desire.

Skimming my lips down her throat, I stop to suckle each of her hard nipples before continuing down the length of her body.

I kiss the birthmark she has on the side of her right hip before skimming downward with deliberate intention. I spread open her legs. Her thighs tremble when I take them in my hands, my mouth hovering above her center.

As I flick my tongue over her clit, she gasps out a trembling plea. "King," she begs breathlessly, "more, please."

I plunge two fingers deep inside finding her G-spot, lapping up her nectar. I plan on feasting on her all day.

"Fuck, your mouth. Keep doing that."

I can't help but chuckle in response before I dive back in and indulge. Every moan, every word, and every reaction from her fuels my desire to give her more. I can tell that she's reached the precipice of her pleasure as a beat of silence overtakes her. Suddenly, I feel her tighten before letting out a deafening scream that echoes off the walls.

"Fuck! Yes! King!" She's experiencing pure ecstasy now, and I'm loving every second of it.

I peel myself away from her to grab a condom, but only after slipping it on do I realize how much I miss being connected to her already. I kneel between her legs and our gaze locks. My anticipation reflected back in her eyes.

Myka breathes heavily as I press against her entrance. "I need you—inside me," she pleads.

"I need to be inside you," I whisper before thrusting into her.

We're locked in an embrace as if we've found home. She clings to me tightly as I move in and out of her, pushing deeper with each thrust to the point it feels like I'm inside her soul.

Thank the gods it was Myka who found me, I think as our bodies become one. I don't know where the fuck that came from, but now is not the time, so I push the thought away.

My hips continue to move in sync with hers until neither of us can take it anymore, blissfully falling into each other's arms in sheer ecstasy.

Maybe I found what will help me pass the time while I'm here.

Chapter Four

Myka

WHEN I MOVED to Luna Harbor to help my grandfather—who was ill at the time—I never thought I would become a jack-of all-trades. Some days I work at the tattoo parlor, others I'm working at the brewery, and nights like this I'm a server at the bar and grill. I'm not complaining about it. In fact, I know I'll miss it once we all go back to our old lives.

If I can find my old life.

I take a deep breath and plaster a smile on my face as I approach the group of five who have just been seated. "Good evening. Welcome to Wicked Luna Bar and Grill. My name is Myka, and I'll be your server tonight. Can I get you started with something to drink?"

As I rattle off the specials for the evening, I notice someone approaching out of the corner of my eye. I turn to see Kingston making his way through the bar. My heart sinks a little, did he come to see me?

What happened with it's a one-time thing?

I should read him *The Myka's Rules of Hookups Book*—when I write it, of course.

He, of all people, knows that it was a one-time deal.

Well, one night.

We parted ways and... why is he here? Don't be so dramatic, Myka. He's probably here to just eat and drink, not to see you. Right?

When I approach the bar, he's chatting with my brother Efren. "Hey there," King says, flashing me a grin.

"Hey, King," I say, trying to keep my tone flat so no one figures out that we hooked up.

"More work and less chat." Efren glances at the other tables. "You can catch up with us later."

"It's not like you're paying me," I say, sticking my tongue out.

"I'll catch up with you later," Kingston says.

"No, you won't. If you need an update about our family, you can come to me," my annoying brother quips.

And maybe this is the right thing to do, stay away from the

eldest St. James. After yesterday, I realized Kingston is dangerous.

He's like a storm.

One you don't see coming, and without warning, he can sweep in before you know it, rocking you to the core.

With his piercing gaze and electrifying touch, he awakened something inside me that I thought was long dead. Which might sound good for one night, but it's bad in the long term. I know his kind. Kingston St. James is one of those men who can leave you bare, shivering, and broken.

I don't need that kind of complication.

I won't go there with him or anyone.

I can't be vulnerable and expose myself again.

I pieced myself together once before—I can't afford to shatter, or if I do, I'll become dust.

So in conclusion, I don't need him.

"Everything okay?" Iskander inquires with an arched brow.

"Yeah, why?"

He gives a nod toward the door. "Earlier today King was here… and according to Efren, spent the whole time gawking at you." He scratches his chin. "Or was it drooling over you."

"Doubtful, and eww. He's too old for me and your friend," I lie with a shrug, mentally crossing my fingers that he won't see through it. "What about you? Are you good?"

He nods, but I can see the doubt in his eyes.

"You should head home with Siobhan and Rumi," I

suggest, changing the topic. Sending him with his girlfriend and their niece is a good way to distract him. "We got everything under control."

"They're with Mitch," Iskander responds abruptly, and adds, "Siobhan and Rumi."

I arch a brow. "We don't like Mitch?"

"He's okay," Iskander says hesitantly, "but he's monopolizing my time with Siobhan. Although, I understand, I prefer to stay away. But I want Rumi to bond with him, and it's hard when I'm around."

"She's a very loving kid," I reassure him. "I'm sure she'll bond with her dad soon. There's no need to stay away." I check the clock on the wall. "Why don't you leave around eight? By then she should be asleep."

Iskander's eyes flicker between me and the door. "Are you sure you'll be okay with that?"

I nod confidently. "Of course I will. Efren and Nando are here, too. If not me, trust your brothers to do their job. You don't have to worry about anything." I give him a reassuring smile.

THERE ARE some advantages to being the only girl among five siblings. They pamper me a lot. Around eleven, my older brother Efren sends me home. Once I get there, I take a long shower and put on my pajamas, then I check my phone. The first things to pop up are my text notifications. Kingston has been blowing up my phone all night.

K. St. James: *Can we have a repeat?*

K. St. James: *It'd be the last time. I'm heading home tomorrow.*

Against my common sense, I respond.

This shocking news hits me by surprise. He and his family have been hiding in Luna Harbor because their sister was allegedly being stalked by a cartel.

Myka: *Why are you leaving? Is it safe for you to go back to Seattle?*

My heart rate races as I wait for him to respond.

K. St. James: *The Organization said it was safe for us to go back home. Though, I'll be anxious until I see my sister again.*

I bite my bottom lip. My gut says she's not okay. Back in another life, I used to work for The Organization. My past involvement with them is something no one speaks of—because I requested it. Back then, I wanted to do everything Manelik, my twin brother, did. I was good until I was captured and… well, let's just say I didn't leave unscathed. I was left with many physical and mental scars. Fortunately, most of the external scarring has disappeared thanks to laser treatments and ointments. But the internal ones sneak back during my dreams, or more like nightmares.

And I understand why Kingston needs the distraction. He needs to forget what could be happening to Teddy.

Myka: *Come to my place.*

K. St. James: *Are you sure?*

Myka: *Of course. It'll be our last hurrah—a goodbye gift from your friendly hostess in Luna Harbor. :wink: emoji.*

K. St. James: *I like how you think. I'll be there in ten.*

Chapter Five

Myka

THREE WEEKS LATER...

Manelik throws a kitchen towel into the box labeled "Donate" and turns to me, arching an eyebrow. "So, what are you going to do with your life, Myk?"

I shrug and try to avoid his all-knowing eyes.

"That's not an answer," he says, pressing his lips into a thin line.

"What do you want me to tell you?" I say, my face heating up with annoyance. "My life was all figured out until our dad demanded we come to Luna Harbor. I no longer have a boyfriend—he didn't like long-distance relationships. I quit my job, and now I'm stuck in limbo, not knowing what to do next."

Manelik raises an eyebrow. "Don't you mean you dumped the deadbeat boyfriend we all hated?"

I nod. He's right. Supporting his art was expensive, and I wasn't getting anything in return, not even sexual favors.

"You chose to quit your job," he reminds me, his arms folded across his chest.

"Well, yes, because freelancing pays a lot more than working for a company," I explain to him.

"It sounds to me like you know what you want, but you're just complaining about something or trying to avoid giving me a straight answer." He gives me a challenging look.

I shrug. "Not really, but you could try going into counseling if this musician gig doesn't work out for you."

"Very funny. What are you going to do with the house?" he asks, his eyes searching mine.

Why is he asking so many questions? I shift my weight from one foot to another, wondering when this interrogation will be over. "Not sure," I respond and add, my voice carrying a tinge of annoyance, "Can I figure that out later?"

I own a house in San Diego that serves as an Airbnb. The income is good, but I might want to sell the place and buy a new property in… well, I have no idea where I want to move.

That's where I'm stuck. I don't know what to do with the rest of my life. Spending a few years close to my brothers was great, but they have their own lives. They always have.

Iskander will be going back to New York with Siobhan.

Manelik will start touring with his band or going back to work full-time for The Organization. Nydia, my best friend and his wife, will be following him whenever it's possible. Efren is leaving for… I don't even know where he's going.

Presumably, Nando is moving to Seattle. However, I can see him heading back to the East Coast with his fiancée, Bri. Where does that leave me? In the middle of a city where I don't have many friends, feeling lonely.

I can do that somewhere else.

"I might travel," I say, fidgeting with the marker. "Being a freelancer has its benefits, like working wherever I want."

He raises an eyebrow, eyeing me curiously. "Are you still getting steady contracts?"

"Yep," I say, forcing a smile and pushing away the annoyance that creeps up my chest. "You don't need to worry about me."

He scoffs. "That's a tall order."

"Well, I'm fine," I insist, hoping to end the conversation.

His eyes bore into mine. "Somehow, I don't believe you."

"But you're going to have to live with what I tell you," I insist.

"Where are you going to live?" he asks, using a softer tone.

"If I'm traveling, it doesn't matter. Though, I have the apartment in Seattle as a home base."

"If you need anything…" he starts, but lets the words trail off.

I smirk confidently. "I'll figure it out."

He shakes his head and opens his mouth to say something else, when he opens the kitchen drawer—what my father likes to call "my black hole"—to reveal a stack of papers. "What's this?" he asks, raising an eyebrow.

"Umm… it's thin, flat material made from fibers obtained from wood pulp or other sources?" I joke, hoping to deflect his attention because I have no idea what he found.

He narrows his gaze, glaring at me. "You're adopting?"

"Uh, that," I say, gulping hard. "It's just a thought for later."

"This is a big commitment," he says, his voice heavy with caution.

I nod. "I know. At least eighteen years, but if I don't screw up, it's going to be a lifetime."

His face creases into a frown.

"Just say it," I prompt him softly. "You want to tell me that I should wait for the right man and have a conventional family."

"I wasn't—" Manelik starts to protest.

"But you were," I cut him off, feeling my temper rising. "We're twins. I know how you think."

He sighs heavily, running a hand through his hair. "Well then, why not wait?"

"Wait for what?" I demand, my voice shaking with emotion. "No one will ever accept me with the darkness in my past and the future I can't promise them."

He pauses and looks up at the ceiling, seemingly measuring his words carefully. "You don't know that," he says tentatively.

"Which part?" I challenge him, my hands clenched in tight fists at my sides.

His gaze softens, and he shakes his head slowly side to side before continuing hesitantly. "Just because Jayden—"

"Don't say his name," I interrupt him, my tone becoming more urgent and angrier. "We don't talk about my past or the people who were a part of it. I've moved on and I'm fine. Maybe it's time for you to accept that."

As I speak, I start pacing back and forth around the kitchen and living room area.

I don't remind him about how, for the past year, I've been hanging out with babies and the new me realized that I want a child. I won't tell him that I already filled out my application. There's no point in discussing what hasn't happened yet—until a child is actually in my arms.

"Sorry, Myk," he apologizes, and I don't know if it's because he's trying to butt into my decisions, or because he couldn't save me in time.

It doesn't matter, though. If only he could understand that I'm no longer broken, just wired differently.

"I'm fine," I assure him, coming to a stop in front of him. "You need to stop worrying about me."

He nods quietly before adding, "Just try to stick around. I hate when you distance yourself from us."

"That's why I'm renting a place in Seattle," I admit, my voice barely audible as one lone tear silently threatens to fall down my cheek. As I wipe it away, I turn toward the window, trying to compose myself.

"Sorry, I didn't mean to upset you," Mane says softly, his hand on my shoulder.

I shrug it off, turn around to face him, and force a smile. "It's okay, I just need you to stop trying to fix me. I don't need fixing—or saving."

My phone buzzes. When I check, it's Kingston St. James sending a text. I walk away so my nosy brother doesn't see it before I unlock the screen.

> K. St. James: My cousin told me he's flying you back to Seattle. Where are you staying?

> Myka: Lang needs to keep his mouth shut.

> K. St. James: True, but that's not why I'm contacting you. Where are you staying?

> Myka: I'm moving to an apartment. I'll send you the address. You can visit me tonight. :wink: emoji.

> K. St. James: Thank you for the invite. I needed it.

> Myka: Any news about Teddy?

> K. St. James: Nothing yet. Seth and Teddy are still MIA.

> Myka: They'll find them.

> K. St. James: I want to believe you, but they're still looking for my brother Archer. He disappeared almost eight years ago.

> Myka: Have faith. I'll see you at nine, bring food.

"Who are you talking to?" Manelik asks.

I glance at him, wondering if he knows where Teddy and Seth are at this moment. The Organization hides a lot of information from the families but not their operatives.

"A friend," I answer casually.

He nods solemnly, and I feel a twinge of worry in the pit of my stomach. "Be careful with your new friend," he warns me, his voice soft and low. "You're a terrible judge of character."

"Thanks for that. But shouldn't you be looking for Seth and Teddy instead of bugging me?" I ask, my voice laced with exasperation.

"My team is off duty while other operatives are searching for them." He shrugs nonchalantly, though his eyes are troubled. "Apparently, we're too close to them to be objective." I offer him a comforting smile, trying to quell the anxious flames in his gaze.

Of course he's too close to the case. Seth is like a little brother to him—and a big part of our family. I'm concerned for them, but I know The Organization always finds their people. Well, except Archer St. James.

"They'll find them," I assure him.

He looks away, whispers something too low for me to hear, and then scans the house around us. "What else do we need to pack?"

"We got everything I need." I pause and ask, "Are you sure you can stay to wait for the movers?"

"Yep," he says, checking his watch. "I'll walk you to the landing strip. The helicopter should be here soon."

"Thank you," I say sincerely, a lump forming in my throat.

"For?" he prompts me, his gaze softening.

"Being a supportive and loving brother."

"Anytime," he states simply, a small smile tugging at his lips as he ruffles my hair affectionately.

We both know there are other things I should thank him for. My mind shifts to Kingston, wondering what my brother would think if he found out I had been seeing him—never mind sleeping with him. He might not care much, but Iskander would not like it one bit.

I'll stop it soon. As soon as Teddy is home and safe, we'll go back to being perfect strangers. Right?

Chapter Six

Current Hookup: It's been a week since the last time we saw each other. I thought you said you'd be back in a couple of days.

Myka: I arrived earlier today. Though, I'm spending the weekend at Mane and Nydia's house.

Current Hookup: Is this a polite way to say: I'm not available for you, Kingston?

Myka: I wasn't thinking about that, but if you were messaging me for a booty call, I'm afraid it's a hard no.

Current Hookup: Can I make an appointment for Monday?

Myka: Then it wouldn't be a booty call.

Current Hookup: Let's call it a scheduled hookup.

Myka: You're changing Myka's Rules for Healthy Hookups.

Current Hookup: Is that even a thing?

Myka: I can make it a thing. It'll be a guide.

Current Hookup: Are you going to include anything in regards to sexting?

Myka: That's a good question. Sexting is always fun. I should make it an entire chapter. Or create a pamphlet. We could sext later tonight.

Current Hookup: Why not SexTime?

Myka: What is that? :raised-eyebrow: emoji.

Current Hookup: Like FaceTime, but with sex. You know, naked, touching… it'll be fun.

Myka: :laughing: emoji.

Myka: We're not making that a thing, but we can discuss the things I want you to do to me the next time I see you.

Current Hookup: Will you be wearing fuck-me heels?

Myka: Sure. What else do you want me to wear?

Current Hookup: Just those and a sexy smile.

Myka: If I do, what will you give me?

Current Hookup: Multiple orgasms, but we probably have to discuss that next time.

Myka: Why?

Current Hookup: I'm at my mother's house—we're having family dinner. It'll be weird if I have to go to my childhood room to jerk off because I'm horny as fuck.

Myka: Can you imagine if I were there? You could drag me along and… I might scream so loud the neighbors would show up at the door and complain.

Current Hookup: Behave.

Myka: What happens if I don't? Are you going to spank me?

Myka: Will you spank me for being a bad girl?

Current Hookup: Bad girls don't get rewarded.

Myka: What kind of reward would I get if I'm a good girl?

Current Hookup: I'll make you come so hard you won't remember your own name.

Myka: Promises, promises.

Current Hookup: Leave your brother's house and I'll show you.

Current Hookup: I'll worship your body all night long.

Myka: Will it be rough?

Current Hookup: Rough, slow, hard, sweet... say yes, and... you'll see.

Myka: Let's meet at my place. Keep yourself all pent up so you can fuck me all night.

Chapter Seven

Kingston

"WHERE ARE YOU GOING?" Myles asks, his voice trailing behind me as I press the elevator button. I spin around to find him standing in the home-office doorway. His tall frame fills it completely.

"You're home?" I ask, trying to dodge his question.

He nods, a smirk on his lips. "Yup. Just came from babysitting Matilda, Arlo, and Slade." He pauses, his eyes narrowing to slits. "Heard you didn't want to pitch in."

"Zach complained about me for not watching his children?

Come on," I scoff, rolling my eyes. "I'm still burning the midnight oil trying to keep up with the work that piled up during our Luna Harbor *trip*."

I look away, avoiding eye contact. You're a fucking liar, St. James. Okay, so maybe using work as a cover for visiting Myka every chance I get is pathetic.

"What happened to taking more breaks and being more with our family?" he teases, a smirk tugging at the corner of his lips.

Myles grins wider, as if he can read my thoughts. "Are you finally going to tell me that you brought yourself a souvenir from Luna Harbor?"

I gulp, taking a step back. "Excuse me?"

"You heard me." He grins mischievously.

"I don't know what you're implying," I reply cautiously, my body growing tense.

"Oh, so you're playing stupid." He shrugs, his smirk widening even further. "Okay, we'll pretend you weren't fuckin' around with Myka Cantú."

The blood drains from my face as the realization hits me like a ton of bricks. "Where did you get that from?" I choke out.

"We saw you," he replies smugly, his grin stretching across his face.

A wave of panic rolls through me. "We? As in you and who else?"

"Fletcher and I saw you," he replies evenly, matching my posture. "That's what happens when a bored football player and an investigative journalist have too much time on their hands."

My jaw drops open in surprise. "Shouldn't you be investigating something else around the world and leave me alone?"

He shakes his head slowly. "Until Teddy is safely home, I plan to stick around."

While our sister was helping The Organization to capture a cartel, she went missing along with Seth Bradley. "Have you heard anything?" I ask, hoping that someone called him and told him she's safe.

"Nope. I talked to Lang earlier today. They're still looking for her," he answers.

I nod a couple of times before summoning some courage to ask, "What about Piper? Have they found her yet?"

Piper Decker has been part of our family since she was four and was engaged to our brother Archer before he… disappeared. Piper was with Teddy when the cartel first attempted to kidnap my sister. She saved Teddy, but after that, no one has heard from her. I'm hoping that she's hiding or… I run a hand through my hair, as I pray that she's okay.

He sighs, the sound echoing through the room. "No. She's probably dead and with Archer."

"Don't say that. They're—" I want to protest, to argue that it's impossible because our brother isn't dead and they just haven't found him yet. After all, Piper was so sure of that, wasn't she? But before I can say any more, Myles holds up a hand.

"Stop," he says firmly, glancing around the room before continuing in a low voice. "I know you, Lang, and Piper still believe he's around. I think it's time we—" He pauses and chuckles quietly, as if he's suddenly recalling a joke and that Teddy and Piper's disappearance doesn't matter. "You know what Lang told me?"

I look up at him expectantly. "Please, enlighten me," I urge him with a pointed look, because maybe he's having a breakdown and I have to commit him to an institution.

"There's apparently a third party involved in this issue"—his voice is barely a whisper now—"and they believe these people are helping The Organization, and they might've rescued Piper."

My eyes go wide. "But we don't know for sure?"

He gives me a grim nod. "They can't find anything," he admits slowly. "But Lang said, 'What if Archer rescued her and is now helping us?'"

I stare at Myles. This sounds insane, like many of our cousin's ideas, but plausible.

"It could be him," I murmur in agreement, knowing our younger brother would do anything for Piper.

He cocks his head, peering at me with skepticism. The roles have changed, and now he thinks I'm the crazy one. I shrug a shoulder. "It's a good theory. We can only hope that they're safe and together."

"Let's move on from this crazy theory and back to you. This thing with Myka Cantú, how serious is it?" His voice is laced with curiosity.

I try to throw him off with a shrug. "We're just having a bit of fun," I respond, feeling the guilt prickle up my throat.

Myka's stunning beauty captivates me—but it's not just

that. She's smart, witty, and has this way of making me feel alive, as if I'm not just a corporate drone.

And yet, the thrill of the forbidden twines with my own yearning desires, and I know I'm betraying someone or something. Soon enough, though, we'll call it off. She travels a lot and I... Well, I'm not exactly looking for a committed relationship.

I'm thinking of hiring her. She's a brilliant designer and having her create the branding for our new line of frozen food might be one of the best decisions I'll make in a long time—if she accepts my offer. I can't give her anything more than this or what we have now. There's no way I can be attached to anyone —I'm not the kind of man who gets attached to anyone or falls in love.

Myles raises an eyebrow. "You know what I was thinking when Fletch and I were staking out Luna Harbor?"

"That we're too old to be roommates and maybe one of us should move out?" I joke, already knowing what he's going to say.

He scoffs. "Nah. I think this setup is great, especially for me. I'm always traveling, so it saves me money. I'm not ashamed to live with my older brother."

"So... Then what were you thinking?" I prompt questioningly.

Myles pauses and sets his gaze on me. "We're too old for one-night stands."

I snort incredulously. "Says the guy who recommended WildMatch."

He shrugs a shoulder. "It's a great app, but don't you want

to settle down? Find 'The One'?"

"Do you?" I challenge him curiously.

He considers this for a moment, and then shakes his head slightly before answering in a quiet voice, "If I find the woman of my dreams, then yes."

"That's what's different between you and me. I don't have dreams."

"Zach's right," he says with a hint of amusement in his voice. "You are a walking tragedy. What, or who, numbed your heart?"

I bark out a laugh, although there's no real humor behind it. "No one," I reply sardonically.

He looks at me skeptically, brows furrowing together in confusion as he inquires, "Then… what the fuck is your deal?"

"What's the point of marriage? You saw what happened to Mom and Dad's relationship. Then there was Zach's first marriage. Even if Archer is alive, Piper has been living with a broken heart…" I trail off, pointing at my chest and adding in a low voice, "And I'm perfectly fine with my fifty-year plan to stay single."

"Then why are you still with Myka?" he asks, as if that's a problem.

"She wants the same thing I do, fun with no attachments," I reply casually, as if it's an obvious answer.

Just then, my phone rings. It's Myka. I respond immediately, because we don't talk, we text. Is there an emergency? "Hey," I greet her.

"She's on her way to Seattle Memorial," Myka whispers urgently.

"Who?" I ask in confusion, unsure of who she is referring to.

"Teddy," she responds solemnly.

"What? How do you know?" I probe, wondering why no one else has called me yet.

"I've got my ways," she replies in a stern voice. "It's your job to protect her. You have to be assertive. Keep any negativity away from her and be supportive. You need to be her shield against anyone who tries to act like they know what she's feeling —including your parents."

I furrow my brow in confusion. "What are you saying?"

Myka takes a deep breath before continuing. "Listen, I don't know what happened to her, but I heard it's bad." She pauses for a moment before adding quietly, "You need to be her rock, okay?"

I swallow hard and say nothing, letting her words sink in.

Myka goes on, "Call me if it gets to be too much for you, and remember that I'm here for you."

"Okay. Thank you." I take a moment to process all the information in my head after hanging up and look at Myles.

"Who was it?" he asks.

"Teddy…" I answer, trying to assimilate Myka's words. "Teddy is heading to Seattle Memorial… Myka wants me to be Teddy's shield and keep away any condescending assholes that might want to hurt her any more than she already is."

A wave of protectiveness surges through me and I resolve that nothing and no one will hurt my little sister ever again.

"Are you sure Teddy is going to the hospital?" Myles asks,

his voice curious and softening with the understanding that something is wrong.

I nod confidently. Myka wouldn't call me out of the blue based on a gut feeling alone.

"Let's go there and be ready for anything. Myka said that Teddy is going to need us."

"We'll be there for her," he agrees.

Chapter Eight

Kingston

MYKA WAS RIGHT. Teddy arrived at Seattle Memorial and was rushed to the operating room. The doctor who came with her didn't give us any information and didn't even acknowledge our presence before she left. In fact, after she'd talked to the medical personnel.

Hoping that she gave some information to The Organization, I approach Grace Bradley, who is not only an agent, but the daughter of one of the owners.

"Were you able to speak to her?" I ask.

Grace frowns.

"The doctor," I answer her silent question.

"Oh, her." Her nostrils flare. "Nope, and I was forced to let her go. She wasn't alone. And we didn't want to get into a fight with members of another agency."

"Another agency?"

She shrugs. "That's just an assumption."

"And Seth? Did they find him?"

Grace emits an exasperated sigh which conveys nothing about her concern for the fate of her brother, but instead, seems more like an annoyance at him. Tilting her head toward the hallway, she proceeds to walk away, and I follow her without a word until we're out of the hospital where Nate—Grace's youngest brother—has already joined us.

How did I not notice him? He moves like a cat—stealthy and almost invisible—a trait the three Bradley siblings have acquired thanks to their training with The Organization.

"Why are we here?" Nate questions, crossing his arms in front of his chest.

"He's asking me about Seth," Grace mumbles under her breath.

"We don't know where he is," he says with exasperation before turning toward Grace and speaking again in a hushed yet firm tone, "Grace, I swore not to say a word. We got Teddy. She's safe. I can't jeopardize…" He groans in frustration before he finishes his sentence, "A mission The Organization hasn't authorized."

She arches an eyebrow as if challenging him. "Where are

your loyalties?" Then points toward the sky. "You didn't let me get any information from the doctor."

Nate snorts. "I'm loyal to our brother. If I want him to get out of his current situation, I have to keep my mouth shut—and you should do the same. If it wasn't for me and my connections, he and Teddy would be dead."

"Piper is dead," she whimpers, and he takes her into his arms.

"She's probably—"

"She's safe," Nate confesses, interrupting her. "Please, I need you to keep this between us."

"Safe like Teddy?" My voice comes out harshly. I point to the hospital and add, "Because my sister is anything but safe. She's broken. Did you see the bruises? She was bathed in blood."

Nate releases Grace and pinches the bridge of his nose. "Believe me, they tried their best to protect Teddy. And yes, Piper is fine."

"So I guess the theory that Archer rescued her is wrong," I scoff, because I had some hope that my brother would be back.

"Who rescued her?" Grace asks. "Who's behind this?"

"Let it go, G. I need you to let me work this one out," Nate says, then turns toward me. "The theory about Archer rescuing Piper isn't wrong, but it's not right, either."

"What does that mean?"

"He's just messing with you," Grace says. "He does that to confuse you and get you to forget whatever we were discussing."

Nate gives her a lopsided smile. "Sure, let's go with that."

Then he turns to look at me, giving me a threatening glare. "Keep this information tight, or you'll find out which one of the Bradley siblings is the most lethal." And with that, he walks away.

I stare at him, dumbfounded, and then look back at Grace. "What was that?"

"A threat."

"But he's Nate," I answer, trying to make sense of what just happened. Sure, he's not the one-year-old kid I encountered when I first met his family. But Nate is usually laid-back, unlike his brother, Seth.

She nods. "Yep, but don't disregard him. He might not kill you in your sleep, but he's the best hacker in The Organization. He could mess with you without leaving home." Grace squeezes my hand. "Sorry about Teddy. I wish…"

"It wasn't your fault."

"My therapist and Nate keep telling me that, but for the second time in my career as an agent, I feel like a failure. Back when I was nineteen, it was a rookie mistake. Now…"

My phone buzzes, and when I look at it, Myka's name flashes. Grace presses her lips together and stares at me. "Be careful with her."

"She's a friend." I show her the phone.

She nods. "Myk pretends to be cold, but she's not. Keep her away from anything related to Teddy."

Instead of telling her that she was the one who informed me my sister was on her way to the hospital, I ask, "Why?"

"This might hit too close to home," she answers and walks away.

One thing is for sure. The Bradley siblings are weird and

cagey. I don't put too much thought into what she said, and I answer the phone.

"Hey," I greet her.

"How is she?"

"She's in surgery," I mumble, closing my eyes and trying not to lose my shit—as I've been doing all night. "But I don't know… how am I supposed to help her?"

"By being there for her," she mumbles. "You'll know what to do. Trust your instincts."

"What should I do with all the people in the waiting room? I doubt she'll want to see them once she's awake."

"Of course, everyone is there. That's the Decker way," she chuckles. "Let them be there for you. Once your sister is awake, they'll leave and come around when she's ready. Trust them to know what they're doing."

"You sound like an expert."

"I've been around them since I was four," she answers. "If you need me…"

"Can you come here?"

"In spirit, yes," Myka answers. "But I can't drive there. Sorry. Text or… come by if you need to speak to me."

"Thank you," I mumble.

"Don't thank me, just reach out if it gets… call me," she says, hanging up.

I'm slightly confused by the conversation. Is there something I'm missing? What is it?

Maybe it's just my imagination. The important thing is that I concentrate on Teddy. The rest isn't as critical. Not until I know she's in a good place.

Chapter Nine

Kingston: Sorry I didn't stay last night. I wanted to make sure everything was ready so I could take Teddy back to my place.

Myka: Some days I feel like we need to discuss the meaning of hookups and the rules. You don't need to justify why you didn't stay. Actually, you don't have to stay the night.

Kingston: Oh, I know that, but I'm also a gentleman.

Myka: That you are. By the way, did I send you the list of therapists for Teddy as you requested?

Kingston: Yes, and Seth sent me one similar too.

Myka: Wait, you talked to Seth? I thought he was MIA.

Kingston: Shit, I forgot that's a secret. Can you please keep that between us?

Myka: Yes, but is he okay?

Kingston: Yes. He's been checking in with me to see how Teddy is doing.

Myka: I hope he doesn't break her heart because of what happened to her.

Kingston: Do you think he would?

Myka: Probably not. He was raised to be a gentleman, like you. Plus, he adores Teddy.

Kingston: No, he doesn't. She's just his best friends' sister.

Myka: Are we talking about Archer or Burke?

Kingston: Both?

Myka: Either way, he's in love with your sister.

Kingston: He better stay away from her.

Myka: If he wants to be close, please allow that. It'll help her to know that, no matter what, someone loves her.

Kingston: Are you sure?

Myka: Trust me.

Kingston: In the past few days, I've noticed you know a lot about trauma. I really appreciate you sharing your knowledge and helping me navigate this treacherous road.

Myka: Glad to help you in any way I can.

Kingston: Is it okay if I swing by your place tomorrow?

Myka: Another booty call, St. James?

Kingston: Actually, I wanted to discuss the designs for the new frozen food line.

Myka: Oh, well… yeah, let me know at what time you'll be here.

Kingston: I will. Thank you for everything.

Myka: Did you seriously just have coffee and a pistachio croissant delivered to my door?

Kingston: Enjoy.

Myka: Rule #3: Don't be swoony.

Kingston: What are rules #1 and #2?

Myka: I don't know, but I feel like there has to be something more pressing, like not falling in love, or don't get attached?

Kingston: Figure those out before you start collecting rules. Anyway… How's the guide book coming along?

Myka: I'll write the book and I might even design the cover today. You'll see, it'll become a thing.

Kingston: I've no doubt that it'll be perfect—and blush pink to match with your outfits.

Myka: Not all my clothes are pink.

Kingston: You're always wearing something pink. Even your accessories.

Myka: Huh… I never noticed that.

Kingston: See you later, beautiful.

Myka: Rule #4: Don't give endearing nicknames to your hookup.

Kingston: Am I still Current Hookup in your contacts?

Myka: No, you were there when I switched it to Kingston—for now.

Kingston: I can't wait to see what you call me next.

Myka: PITA

Kingston: Like the bread or the character from The Hunger Games?

Myka: More like pain in the ass. Good luck with Teddy.

PITA: It's been… I lost count of how many days, but Teddy is still not talking.

Myka: Give her time.

PITA: How long?

Myka: As much as she needs. Trust the process and don't force it.

PITA: Thank you for coming to my office earlier.

Myka: Don't tell anyone, but I always wanted to get fucked against a window in the CEO's office.

PITA: Really?

Myka: No, but it was exciting. The entire lunch hour was... different and fun.

PITA: After you left, I thought of something dirty I want to try. Come by tomorrow and I'll show you.

Myka: I might buy something really sexy and be your 10 o'clock, Mr. St. James.

PITA: Fuck, we need to stop. I'm driving home and can't stop at your place for a quickie.

Myka: You're texting and driving? :rage: emoji.

PITA: I'm texting by voice. I would never text and drive.

Myka: Still, I'll cut this short. Only I'm allowed to see that you're hard and ready for me.

PITA: Are we being a little possessive, Ms. Cantú?

Myka: Nope. Rule #5: We don't belong to each other, therefore, we shouldn't be possessive.

PITA: I'm home. I'll talk to you later.

Myka: Call if you need me.

PITA: Thank you for always being there for me.

Chapter Ten

Kingston

Sex is not the answer.

I want it. I need it. I crave it.

But sex is not the... Who am I kidding? I need sex before I go insane. I can feel the restlessness buzzing inside me.

Teddy's been home for two weeks, but it feels like an eternity. My sister arrived mentally and physically battered.

The light that used to shine so brightly in her eyes is gone, leaving her desolated and shattered. I don't know how to fix her, how to piece her back together—how to bring her back to life. All I know is that I have to try to be there for her.

I'm doing my damn best to shield her from the world and give her everything she needs. I'm her big brother, her protector, and I'll do whatever it takes to keep her safe. But it's not enough. Nothing seems to be enough.

It kills me to see her like this, to see the pain etched into every line of her face. She's just a shadow of the girl she used to be, and my heart is crumbling. I wish I could take away her pain. I wish I could make everything alright again. But I know it's impossible.

She doesn't want to talk about what happened to her, and I don't blame her. I can see the fear in her eyes. I listen to her screams at night when she's asleep, reliving the worst moments of her life. She doesn't talk about what happened, but we know what those monsters did to her. It tears me apart inside to think about what she went through.

I wish I could take her pain away, but I know I can't. All I can do is be there for her, to hold her when she needs to cry, and to listen when she wants to talk. I'll do whatever it takes to help her heal, to make her feel safe and loved again—because that's what big brothers do.

As I'm pacing around the kitchen, fixated on my phone, I hear Myles come up behind me. "You should go out," Myles suggests. "I'll stay here to watch Teddy."

I shake my head. "No way. She needs us both."

"We could call someone else, if you want two people to be with her." He pauses, trying to smile, but he fails. "I might not be as entertaining as you, but I can handle myself."

I scoff. "Everyone knows I'm the boring one of all the siblings. And leaving would be irresponsible," I say. "We made a commitment to Teddy."

"But we don't have to be here twenty-four seven," he says. "And we both know if we call anyone, I'm sure they'll be here at a moment's notice."

But who can we call? Myles and I are the best choices to take care of her. Zach has a pregnant wife and three little ones to care for. Burke has plenty with Chloe's pregnancy. Fletcher is managing his sponsorships—whatever that means.

"Teddy kept you up all night," he remarks. "I'd advise you to take a nap, but it would be best if you use the time to see *your friend.*"

"Myka might not be in town," I respond. Yet, to be honest, I'm prepared to drive to Luna Harbor if that's where she is.

"Text her," he prompts me.

I could argue with him, but instead I follow his suggestion.

> Kingston: Are you in town?

> Myka: Is this another booty call?

> Kingston: Would it upset you if it was?

> Myka: Sex with you is great. Why would I be upset if you want to swing by and fuck me? I asked, because I wanted to see if I had to open my laptop to look at the designs I sent you a week ago, or shave.

> Kingston: Why don't we take a shower together, and I shave you? :grin: emoji.

> Myka: So, you want to clean me up so you can dirty me up all night?

> Kingston: That's the plan.

> Myka: Fine, see you in twenty minutes. Bring me some food, please. I've been so busy, I forgot to eat lunch.

> Kingston: That's it. I'm going to start sending you lunch every day.

> Myka: You don't have to. Actually, you should stop sending breakfast. Rule #7: Don't feed your hookup.

> Kingston: So you don't want me to bring food right now?

> Kingston: And I think that's #6. I lost count.

> Myka: Ugh… bring food and we'll discuss the rules later.

"I take it you're leaving," Myles says as I put away my phone.

"Are you sure it's okay?" I ask one more time. "Because I won't be back until tomorrow morning."

Though Myk says it doesn't matter to her, I don't like to just leave in the middle of the night. It doesn't feel right.

"We'll be fine. I might just binge-watch movies with Teddy all night." He walks toward the pantry and grabs the popcorn kernels. "I'll even prepare some snacks."

"Thank you for doing this."

"She's my sister too, you know," he says. "And we're not your responsibility."

But ever since I was a child, I took my role as their big brother seriously. Once I realized our parents had other more important things to worry about, I made it my mission to ensure they were okay.

And maybe this is one of the reasons why I prefer to stay single. I don't have time for more, I have plenty of other responsibilities.

I TAKE A DEEP BREATH, then rap my knuckles against her door, my heart racing.

The moment Myka opens the door, I'm struck by her stunning beauty. Her long dark hair is flowing over her smooth shoulders, and I love it when she wears tank tops. They show off her gorgeous skin.

Her deep blue eyes pierce into my soul as she looks at me. She understands my pain, and her sad smile seems to confirm that. It's like she knows everything that's going on in my head and heart. I can't help but feel a sense of comfort in her presence. It's as if she's saying, "I know it hurts, but you'll get through this."

Her gaze still lingers on me, and I realize that I'm not alone in this. She's here with me, and that's enough to make me feel like I can face anything.

"Come on in," she says, licking her lips seductively and flashing me a grin. "I'm ready to jump in the shower after we're done with the takeout."

My gaze roams her body, mesmerized by her and I feel my nerves dissipate. The rest of the world fades away when I'm near her. I hold out the bag of takeout, smiling warmly. "I remembered that you love Thai curry with a creamy coconut sauce."

Myka gives me a grateful smile and her eyes light up in delight. "You're incredible," she says, taking the bag from me.

Before we sit down to eat, I pull her into a warm embrace, wrapping my arms around her and breathing in the sweet scent of her hair. "It's so good to see you, beautiful," I say softly.

She looks up at me, her smile giving her eyes an extra sparkle. "It's good to see you too, St. James," she replies.

I lean in, my breath hot on her lips. I feel a spark as our mouths connect, and I can't help but smile. "I thought we agreed you'd call me Mr. St. James," I whisper, unable to resist the pull between us.

She giggles, pushing a lock of hair behind her ear. "We'll see after dinner if you deserve to be called that," she teases, her eyes twinkling with mischief.

I take in her cozy apartment, the bright colors and comfy blankets adding to the intimate atmosphere. "I like this place. It feels so you," I murmur, admiring the paintings and photographs adorning the walls. They evoke a sense of warmth and homeliness.

"Thank you." She beams, her eyes glowing with pride. "I put a lot of effort into making it feel like home."

The décor is laced with shades of pink and peach, and the living room is filled with an array of furry throw pillows and blankets. In the corner, a record player pleases my ears with a familiar melody. It's Too Far From Grace. Manelik is the drummer, and my cousin Lang represents them.

"Do they pay you for the free publicity?" I joke, pointing to the speakers.

A hearty chuckle escapes her lips as she shakes her head. "Nah, but don't tell him I listen to his music," she says with a mischievous grin.

"Why am I not surprised that you love to irritate your older brother?" I tease.

Myka feigns outrage, planting her hands firmly on her hips. "Excuse me, sir, but Manelik isn't older than me. I was born two minutes earlier," she says with a sharp nod.

"Ah, two minutes makes a big difference," I reply.

"It certainly does. How's Teddy doing?" she asks with genuine concern.

I let out a deep sigh. "She's finally speaking," I say, thankful for how far my sister has come.

"That's a huge step. I hope you celebrated," Myka says with a warm smile.

"Just as you recommended," I reply, admiration filling my voice. "How do you know so much?"

"I worked with The Organization for a couple of years," she answers in a hushed tone as if divulging a secret.

"That's a dangerous job," I comment, my brows furrowing in concern.

"Hence, why I quit, and why we shall never discuss it." She gives me a thin smile before digging into her food. After she's done with two bites, she looks up from her plate and says, her voice laced with mirth, "Let's talk about something else. How are the rest of the St. Jameses?"

The way she changes the conversation sounds natural, but there's something in her tone that tells me she's the one uncomfortable with it. I could push for more, to try and figure out what's bugging her, but I don't. We hook up to forget what's happening around us—to be free for a few hours.

My gaze softens. "I'm sure they're doing just fine," I answer, my voice just as light and humorous as hers. We both know the truth of our relationship—fuck buddies.

Then why does this moment feel like anything but that? We've found a kind of blissful stillness in each other's company. Maybe it's time for us to stop this, but can I do it?

Can I just let her go?

Chapter Eleven

Myka

I LEAD us to the bathroom, my heart pounding. As soon as the door clicks shut, Kingston pins me against it and his skillful lips press firmly against mine. Our tongues swirl in perfect harmony. As always, he dominates the kiss—and me. I moan against his mouth, sucking on his bottom lip. Heat spreads through every cell of my body, igniting the desire.

"I thought we were taking a shower?" I gasp between pants, but he's too preoccupied—or too aroused—to respond. His wicked gaze is focused on my clothing, his hands frantically stripping me of it.

His voice, low and seductive, sends a quiver down my spine. I look up to find a charming smile painted on his lips, and I can feel his gaze move to my own before the corner of his mouth curls up. He begins to slowly unbutton his shirt.

I can't help but admire the contours of his body, his defined chest. Instinctively, my hands trace his rippled abs. "Are we in a rush, St. James?" I whisper, feeling my breath hitch.

"It's *Mr. St. James* to you." He crushes his mouth to mine once again, lifting me off my feet, and carries me to the bedroom, setting me on the bed. In one swift move, he removes my panties, and his mouth is at my center, hovering just above my skin. His breath teases my core.

"What do you say?" he murmurs, his face so close to my pussy. The question, combined with his heated gaze, makes my entire body shudder with anticipation.

"Please," I whisper, my voice barely audible. "I need you, Mr. St. James."

My heart thunders in my chest and my body trembles. His heated gaze locks with mine just before he brushes his thumb over my clit, sending waves of pleasure throughout my body.

I press my hips forward, silently begging for more. He slides his fingers inside me, pumping slowly as his mouth ravishes my pussy.

"Faster," I moan.

"I'm in charge, my good girl. I'll reward you soon," he says in a low tone before licking my clit.

Heat rushes to my head, making me dizzy. I'm throbbing

for him, craving for him to make me come as he sucks my clit, curling his fingers inside me. I can feel my orgasm building as I tremble and my vision begins to blur. I finally succumb to a blissful pleasure like never before.

He stands and strips off his jeans and boxers, then rolls on a condom. Without further ado, he covers my body with his big frame and slides every inch of his rock-hard cock into me, letting out a loud growl. He kisses me fiercely, and his hands find their way up and down my body, worshiping it. My fingers trace every hard muscle of his back, and I sway with every thrust. The synchronicity is divine. He moans against my throat, and I grasp onto his biceps as the buildup threatens to consume my entire being.

A strangled grunt escapes his throat that makes my whole body vibrate, releasing a surge of energy that pushes me to the heights of ecstasy.

"You're so beautiful," he murmurs against my skin, rocking against me with increasing speed as his lips rest against the side of my neck.

"Kingston." I moan as his name escapes my lips.

We stay silent while catching our breath in each other's embrace.

As I watch Kingston sleep, I can't help but feel a pang of pain. They call them ghost pains. I'm not hurting, but the scars in my soul remind me of the past. Only those familiar with the aftermath of trauma can understand the unbearable ache of those pains. No amount of therapy can cure them.

Thinking of what Teddy went through brings back a lot of memories. At least she has King to be with her. I stroke his soft hair a few times and kiss his jawline. His peaceful expression contrasts sharply with the turmoil in my own mind. Memories of my own personal hell flood back to me, threatening to drag me under once again.

I know I'm not broken—at least not in the traditional sense—but that doesn't mean I'm not scarred. The marks left by my experiences run deep, and they're a constant reminder of what I've been through. Sometimes it feels like everyone can see them, like they're written all over my body for the world to see.

Therapy has helped me learn how to cope. I manage well enough, but maybe I need to stop helping Kingston with Teddy since it's a reminder of my past. He has a family to support him —and her. I should just step away and live my life. These hookups have to stop before we become more. I have to do it for his sake.

He's getting attached, becoming addicted to the afterglow. Thankfully, I'm not doing the same. I'm smart enough to keep my heart safe.

Do I like that he sends me breakfast every day?

The simple gesture of him sending me breakfast every morning feels like an early morning hug, a reminder that I'm not alone in this world. But with every sweet message and thoughtful gesture, I wonder if he's trying to compensate for something, or if he's expecting something in return. It's possible that he's just a genuinely caring and thoughtful person who wants to have fun.

Any other woman would be falling madly in love with him and would want to trap him. I know better. I can't believe it's real. I know what happens at the end of the chapter. My heart will get shattered into a million pieces. Long ago, I promised myself that I'll never get caught in the never-ending cycle of love and fear.

I won't cling to that hope that this can become something beautiful and real. It's for the best that I delete his number and push him away.

My phone buzzes and I reluctantly push aside my comforter. I take the call in the living room, dragging my feet along the floorboards.

"Yeah?"

"Hey, Myk, it's Lang, your favorite person in the world. How are you?" His voice is low, maybe cautious.

I roll my eyes, knowing he's calling to ask me for a favor. "I'm well, my second to last favorite person in the world. I would fill the silence with pleasantries, but let's cut the crap—what do you want?"

"It's about Teddy," he replies, more serious than before.

"How is she doing?" I ask, my voice softening, as I pretend I have no information on her well-being.

"She's not willing to leave the apartment, so we were thinking…" Lang trails off.

"Nah, don't even finish that sentence," I interject, knowing where it was going.

"You haven't heard me out yet."

"Nope, I don't need to," I reply firmly.

"But you know what she lived through."

"True, but she needs professional help, not me," I answer, my tone suddenly hardening.

"Fair enough, but… I have something else to discuss," he says in an even more serious tone.

I let out an annoyed sigh. "What now?"

"Can you tell me what's happening with you and King?"

I scoff. "Nothing."

Lang pauses before continuing. "Myka, you two have been…" His words trail off and I'm surprised at his sudden hesitation. He's just as blunt as I am. Why is he being cautious with this?

"Fucking. We're fucking. It was great, but it's coming to an end," I say, matter-of-factly.

"I was going to ask you if you can keep it up at least until we're able to send Teddy to rehab," he says.

I raise an eyebrow. "Oh… that's a strange request, but I can manage."

"Good, and can you please do me another favor?"

"I can try."

"Don't break his heart," Lang says.

I laugh, incredulous. "I doubt he would fall for me. Especially if he knew," I reply, a hint of bitterness in my voice.

"Would you like a number for a therapist? I'll pay for it. We can see if someone can thaw your heart," he adds, sarcasm heavy in his words.

I clench my jaw, feeling my temper rising. "I'm good. My

heart is fine on ice. Easier to keep track of the pieces that way. Anything else?"

"Just FYI, Manelik heard the conversation. Sorry, but you decided to announce that you were fucking my cousin," he replies, not sounding apologetic.

"Great. I think I hate you both," I say before hanging up the phone.

When I turn around, I notice Kingston standing in the hallway. He points to the phone. "Who was that?"

"It was Lang," I sigh.

King frowns. "What did he want?"

"Somehow, he found out about us, and Manelik knows too," I say. "We should probably call it quits."

He rolls his eyes. "It's none of their business what we're doing. Unless… do you care? Is this a way to tell me 'lose my number'?"

I shake my head. "Nah. Though I'm leaving for San Diego next week and I'll be gone for a while."

"What for?"

"I'm selling my house, and there's a lot I have to do before it goes on the market," I say, not telling him more.

The house needs a serious renovation. Having it as an Airbnb paid off, until I saw all the cosmetic and structural stuff that was damaged because of all the people who stayed there. It's going to take me months to fix it. Months.

"Text me when you're back," he says, his expression unreadable.

"I'll probably take a vacation afterward." A sly smile forms on my lips. Maybe I am trying to find an excuse to call this off.

I would be fine with it if my twin brother didn't know about it, but now… I can hear Manelik lecturing me about one thing or another. If this gets to Iskander's ears, it'll bet messy.

King quirks an eyebrow. "Are you trying to find a way to avoid me?"

"Nope. I'm telling you about my schedule for the next few months. If you want to drop by San Diego, or come with me when I go on vacation… you're welcome to join. I can always use a plus-one when I travel." I look at him sternly. "Just keep this casual. Nothing heavy, or it's over."

He smirks. "I like you and your I-don't-give-any-fucks attitude. So what did you promise my cousin, then?"

A playful grin spreads across my face. "That I won't break your heart."

He laughs. "No worries there, I don't have one." He winks.

I wish I could have a long-lasting relationship with him. This is a perfect arrangement, isn't it?

Chapter Twelve

Myka

"So, you and Kingston St. James are a thing, huh?" Nydia, my best friend and my twin's wife, sucker punches me with her question.

I stare at the camera, arching an eyebrow and shooting her a "really?" kind of look. "I thought you called for something important, not for a gossip session."

"I'm checking on you. I heard that you moved to San Diego. What happened to sticking close to family?" she probes, her cheerful face completely devoid of any guilt.

"You're too nosy for your own good," I tell her teasingly, pointing the camera at my disaster-ridden house. "As you can see, I'm staging the house so I can put it up for sale."

"Oh, so you're not avoiding us—or Kingston?" she presses on.

I shake my head and laugh. "Nope. I'm just making sure people pay top dollar for this beachfront property. According to my real estate agent, my style is too particular. Buyers these days want neutral colors and minimalist décor."

Her expression morphs from shocked to amused as she nods in agreement. "That sounds boring."

"You understand me. This is why I left. I don't care if Mane knows I'm having fun with the eldest St. James."

"But you didn't tell me about Kingston or your decision to adopt a kid. I had to learn you were doing him from your brother." She narrows her gaze. "What's that about?"

I exhale a deep breath before replying. "The first one doesn't really matter. We were having fun. And the second one… I don't want to jinx it, you know?"

She nods understandingly and smiles sympathetically. "Is there anything I can do to help with the adoption or…?"

"Thea Decker has my application. I already sent in the video interviews, financial information, and… Well, everything they asked for. Hopefully, someone will choose me—that is, if they don't think I'm a crazy person." I shrug, hoping she won't interrogate me about why I'm not waiting for Prince Charming to rescue me from my loveless life.

She might be my best friend, but I doubt she'll understand why I'm not holding my breath or waiting for love.

Nydia doesn't know about Jayden or the past—the hellhole I fell into, or the nightmare I lived. I thought I was in love with him, but he left me. He walked away when I was at my lowest, when I was empty and broken, and wanted nothing more than to stop existing.

I needed him so desperately, but he left me with a shattered heart and a wounded soul.

The anger at his departure still burns fiercely within me. How could he leave me when I needed him the most? How could he just walk away without a second thought, leaving me to pick up the shattered pieces of my life all on my own?

I loved him with everything I had, and yet he still chose to leave.

He left me to face the world alone, with nothing but a broken heart and a wounded soul. And now, even though the seasons have passed, I still can't bring myself to love again. Because the memories of his abandonment remind me that love isn't worth the pain and heartache that comes with it.

Nydia stares at me for several beats before asking, "Did you apply to any other agency?"

I stare at my phone, wondering if I should do it. Thea runs a shelter for pregnant teenagers, helping them with housing and jobs, and if they're not ready to be mothers, she helps them find good homes for their babies.

"What are you thinking?" she inquires.

"She's the best choice," I finally speak, feeling sure of my decision. "Plus, if the mom wants an open adoption, we'll be close to her."

"So you're planning on sticking around," she confirms, hopefulness in her voice.

"Of course," I reply hastily. "This doesn't mean I won't keep traveling and doing my thing—but I'll be there. Maybe even buy a house, too."

"Really?" She raises her eyebrows in curiosity.

I nod, almost afraid that she'll offer me the number of her realtor, or buy the house next door to hers so we can be neighbors. I love my best friend, but living next to my brother isn't my idea of a good time. "Yes," I answer hesitantly. "But the first step is to get rid of this one."

"You could sell it to me," she suggests with a glint in her eye. "I love the place."

I purse my lips and give her a suspicious look. "Do you, now? Knowing you, you just want me to get this over with so I can go back to Seattle right away."

She purses her lips, and a mischievous smile creeps onto her face. "C'mon, I just want my bestie close to me," she singsongs sweetly.

"You're worse than my brother," I reply, rolling my eyes.

"I said, I just want my bestie close to me," she repeats innocently, batting her lashes. "It has nothing to do with your overprotective brother."

"Siobhan is close enough," I remind her, not wanting to discuss her crazy husband. I adore my brother, but he can be too overbearing. "So how's Rumi doing?" I ask, changing the subject.

Siobhan has been caring for her niece, Rumi, while her sister is in the hospital. We're hoping that she'll get better.

While I was in Luna Harbor, I helped babysit the cute toddler. Little Rumi was the one who made me want to start a family of my own. Nydia had wanted me to fall in love with and marry Rumi's father, Mitch, but that man needs a woman to put him back together after the ugly separation and his ex-wife fighting for her life. He doesn't need me to drag him to the seven circles of hell. Hopefully, one day he'll find someone who'll love him and his sweet daughter.

"You could call Mitch and check on them," Nydia suggests.

"Can we stop this ridiculous cupid-matchup campaign?" I groan. "The man might lose the love of his life. He went through a nasty divorce and… give it a few years and you can try to set him up with… anyone but me."

"What's the fun in that?" she teases playfully.

"The last time I checked, I'm not here for your entertainment." I laugh softly. "Which reminds me… I have to continue with my project. Unless…" I pause. "Do you have any updates about Teddy or Piper?"

"I heard Piper is back home, but she's not speaking to anyone but her family. Teddy…" She shrugs. "You might want to ask Kingston."

"We had sex a couple of times and it's over," I tell her before she comes up with some weird story about us dating. "At least they found her—that's all that matters." I sigh, wanting a change of subject. "Why don't you fly down here and help me out?"

"I'm a chemist, not a decorator." She smirks.

"Fine, don't come over." I throw my hands up in mock defeat. "I'll talk to you soon."

"Later." She waves before disappearing from the screen.

When I look at the texts that arrived while I was on the phone with her, I notice one from Kingston.

We're taking Teddy to a rehab center. I have work to do, but send me your address. I might swing by in a few weeks.

As I read the message a few times, my heart races with a mix of excitement and trepidation. Which it shouldn't, because King and I are just having fun. A wise woman would ignore the message.

Part of me knows I should bury my phone or delete the message. Erase his number from my contacts—block him from my life. But the other part, the part that loves his touch, his mouth, and his body, is tempted.

Tempted to play with fire, to see if the flames still burn as bright as they did in Seattle. I know better, but the lure of what he offers is hard to resist. And so, with a few quick taps on my phone, I send him my address.

As I hit send, a wave of uncertainty washes over me.

Am I making a mistake? But it's too late now. I can't help but wonder if it's worth it.

Is it worth it playing with fire, knowing that one of us might get burned?

Just keep it simple, I tell myself. Be cold and teach him that he won't get more than great sex and a few laughs.

I can do that. I'm good at pretending I'm cold and hollow.

Chapter Thirteen

Kingston

"W%%E ALL NEED%% to go to therapy," Myles suggests as we arrange for Teddy to go to rehab.

"You do," Seth, who is still on the phone, agrees from afar.

"Shut up, fucker," I grumble. "You're the one who put my sister in danger."

"Technically, it was Archer," Seth retorts, invoking my dead brother's name. "He's the one who filed the marriage license."

"You're seriously using someone who's no longer with us as an excuse?" I growl incredulously.

He laughs sarcastically. "Dude, one day you'll remember this conversation and apologize. In the meantime, just make sure you add the fake name I gave you as her husband."

"I still don't understand why we're using fake names," I reply warily.

"It's for security reasons," he explains tersely.

"Anyway, when are you coming back?" I ask him.

"Not sure, but hopefully soon," he responds vaguely. "In the meantime, do what Myles said and get yourself a therapist."

"Again, this is your fault," I say firmly. "My only therapy would be if I can beat the shit out of you, Bradley."

"You can try," he snarls menacingly.

Myles sighs audibly. "Children, stop arguing. We need to focus on Teddy now. Going to therapy isn't just about what happened to her—there are other factors at play, too—like our parents' divorce…" His voice trails off, and his face darkens as he remembers the painful truth. We've never discussed this among ourselves, and certainly not with Seth, either.

Mom finally opened up to us and shared her story—a friend of Dad's had raped her, and the trauma was too much for them to handle separately or together. They destroyed each other instead—taking us into their little hell along with them.

"If anything, do it for your future wife and children," Seth says.

I snort. "The ones I don't plan on having."

"Exactly, but your issues don't matter," he mumbles. "Let's focus on your sister. I'll be there tomorrow to fly you to Oregon and back. Please don't tell Teddy I'm the pilot, okay?"

"That's a weird request, but we'll be able to accommodate you," Myles responds.

"Why are we including him on this?" I question after Seth's call disconnects.

"He cares," Myles mumbles. "I know you can't see it, but he loves Teddy."

I scoff. "He had a great way of showing it."

"Go to therapy, and you might learn to forgive him," Myles suggests and then adds, "Not that there's much to forgive. Seth didn't do anything wrong."

I stare at him, confused. Seriously, it sounds as if he's on another wavelength. We used to agree on a lot of things, and since he went to therapy, we can't agree on anything. When his phone buzzes, he leaves my office without another word.

Another glance to the list of therapists Thea Decker sent makes me wonder if I'm the one doing something completely wrong. But you know what can help more than therapy? Sex.

Not only sex. Myka.

Sex with Myka, after enduring these past few weeks, should solve my problems. I grab my phone and fire up a text.

> PITA: My sister is heading to rehab.

> Myka: You said she was in your last text. Did you force her, or is this something she decided to do on her own?

> PITA: We weren't forcing her. It was an intervention. We were trying to convince her to start her life back up.

Myka: :expressionless: emoji.

PITA: We thought it was a good idea.

Myka: It wasn't. You don't give deadlines after a tragedy. You give time and love.

PITA: I listened to you after we fucked up.

Myka: Thank you for listening.

PITA: How's the renovation of your place going?

Myka: Not as great as I thought. There's a lot to do. I might take a break, go to a beach far away, and come back to finish.

PITA: Aren't you in San Diego?

Myka: Uh-huh.

PITA: There's probably a beach close to you.

Myka: I have a beachfront property. What's your point?

PITA: You have a beach. Why would you want to go somewhere else?

Myka: I wish there was a glare emoji—no, a laser-beam emoji. No, I wish there was an app that I could use so I could zap you from the comfort of my home when you piss me off.

PITA: I'm just stating the fact that you don't have to travel to go to a beach.

Myka: It's like telling me that I have food in my fridge and, therefore, I shouldn't go to a restaurant where I can take a break from cooking.

PITA: You want me to visit and cook for you?

Myka: No, I want to go to a different beach.

Myka: Do you even know how to cook real food?

PITA: What do you cook? Plastic?

Myka: I'm just wondering, since you're too pretty and wealthy to do your own laundry—or make your bed.

PITA: There's nothing wrong with having a housekeeper.

Myka: You could do your own laundry.

PITA: We're never going to agree on this, are we?

Myka: Probably not.

PITA: So where do you want me to take you?

Myka: :raised-eyebrow: emoji.

PITA: You want to go on vacation. How about Hawaii? There's also Fiji, Anse Source d'Argent, and Elafonissi Beach.

Myka: All great options. Are you inviting me on vacation?

PITA: Does that go against your rules?

Myka: Rule #8: Never go on a romantic getaway with your hookup.

PITA: I'm not taking you to Paris. I'm dragging you to a beach… maybe I should take you to a private beach where swimsuits are optional.

Myka: But I want someone to pamper me.

PITA: If I promise to pamper you?

Myka: When are we leaving?

PITA: I'll send you all the information via email.

Myka: You might be the best hookup I've ever had in my entire life.

PITA: Ditto.

Myka: By the way, did you choose a therapist?

PITA: Not you too.

Myka: Who else is reminding you to take care of yourself?

PITA: I thought you were going to take care of me, Ms. Cantú.

Myka: Don't try to divert this conversation with sex. After your conversation with your mom, it's important that you go to therapy.

PITA: Rule #10: Don't meddle in the other person's mental health.

Myka: Look at you, learning how to use the rules, but you still have to do it. Not for anyone but yourself.

PITA: Can I think about it?

Myka: Of course. I don't want you to go until you're ready.

PITA: Thank you.

Myka: For?

PITA: Sticking around while I'm dealing with everything that my family and I are going through.

Myka: Happy to do it.

PITA: See you this weekend, then? I'll have the jet ready to pick you up.

Myka: Looking forward to spending some time with you.

PITA: Are we going to sext between now and then?

Myka: Nope, but I'm leaving you with one thought... me tied up and you doing all the things you want with me.

PITA: Fuck, I'm hard... you'll pay for leaving me with that image. Don't touch yourself until we meet, dirty girl.

Chapter Fourteen

Myka

I TAKE A DEEP BREATH, trying to steady my racing heart as I walk closer to Kingston St. James. He's too pretty and perfect to be real.

Control your hormones, I order myself as I walk toward him. He's the epitome of a playboy billionaire, and this affair is anything but serious. Though I anxiously await what he has prepared for us.

"Hey, gorgeous," he rasps, his eyes crinkling with his smile.

Before I can respond, he leans down and captures my lips in a passionate kiss.

Sparks ignite under my skin, and warmth floods through my veins as I part my lips for him. The taste of his lips is like sweet honey, and the warmth of his breath on my face is intoxicating. My mind races as my body responds, and I'm lost in the moment, lost in the feel of his kiss. I'm completely under his spell, lost in a sweet symphony of sensations.

He moves away suddenly, leaving me breathless and wanting more. An ache pulses through my chest from the emptiness, but also a thrill from being with him.

"What was that?" I ask, rubbing my still-tingling lips with the tip of my thumb.

He winks at me and grins. "Just a taste," he replies. "You ready to head out?"

"Are you going to tell me more about our vacation?" I inquire.

He shakes his head, taking my hand in his. We walk toward an imposing private jet, larger than the one that flew me here from San Diego. "How many planes do you own?" I dare to ask.

"Not many. This one used to be Archer's," he informs me. "Piper got it for him on his twentieth birthday. It's part of the fleet now, but we don't use it very often."

I whistle in surprise. "Who gives their fiancé a plane for their birthday?"

He grins almost proudly. "Those two always tried to gift each other big, flashy things they could use in the future. Strange, but romantic too, right?"

I shrug, my mind still reeling at the thought of such an extravagant gesture. We climb up the stairs and enter a luxurious cabin—all cream leather seats and tourmaline blue lighting overhead. "Wow. It looks like a home inside here."

His eyes twinkle with amusement as he takes in my awe-filled expression. "Yep. It's comfortable enough for long trips and has a fuel tank big enough to make transcontinental flights."

I glance at him. "So, where are we going?"

"Lanai," the pilot responds, and Kingston scowls at him.

I ignore his change of mood and clap my hands excitedly. "I love Hawaii. I've never been to Lanai, though."

He kisses my cheek affectionately. "You're gonna love it." He smiles warmly before gesturing to the plush seats around us, adding, "Why don't we get comfortable?"

We take our time to find the perfect spot. I adjust my seat belt and wait for the pilot—or flight attendant—to tell us we're ready for takeoff.

"You ready for this?" King asks, voice low and husky.

"Ready as I'll ever be," I reply, hoping he doesn't notice I'm afraid of takeoffs. "Of course, I would be even more ready if you told me what we'll be doing there."

"And spoil the surprise?" He winks at me.

"More like stoke the anticipation," I correct him.

He laughs and looks out the window at the same time the pilot announces we're cleared for takeoff. My stomach flips, and the butterflies have nothing to do with King and everything with my fears.

As I close my eyes, his hand takes mine. "It's going to be

okay. We're just going for a little ride among the clouds," he says.

As we ascend higher into the sky, I can feel my heart beating faster and my breath becoming shallow. But King's hand in mine is a calming presence, and I lean into him for comfort.

"Look outside, Myk. You don't want to miss this moment."

Hesitant, I open one eye and gawk. The view from above is breathtaking, and I can't help but let out a gasp of awe. King chuckles and pulls me closer to him, his arm draped around my shoulders.

"I knew you would love it," he says, his voice low and sultry. "You look so beautiful up here, surrounded by the clouds."

I blush at his compliment, feeling the warmth spreading through my body. I turn to face him, our eyes locking in a gaze that sends shivers down my spine.

"Thank you," I whisper, my voice barely audible above the roar of the engine. "For bringing me here, for making me feel so alive."

King leans in, his lips hovering just inches away from mine. "It's always fun to make you feel alive," he says, his voice husky with desire.

He closes the distance between us, his lips brushing against mine in a gentle, teasing kiss. I respond eagerly, my heart racing with excitement. Everything around is forgotten.

The moment we're told we can move around the cabin, he invites me to one of the bedrooms. Confession time: I've never had sex on a plane. I'm about to become part of the mile-high club. Kingston shouldn't be my first, but here we are, fulfilling another fantasy.

Kissing, undressing, touching—fucking hard.

And sometimes it feels like he's trying to claim my soul and bury himself deep inside my heart.

As I LIE HERE, tangled up in the sheets and caught in the aftermath of one of the most passionate encounters we've shared, I can't help but feel conflicted. I know the rules of hookups, the unspoken agreement that this is just a casual fling with no strings attached. And yet, as I look at a sleepy Kingston lying next to me, I can't help but feel a sense of longing and a desire for something more.

It's now that I think of the most important rules:

Rule #1: Don't expect anything.

Rule #2: Never wish for more.

Kingston isn't someone I can allow myself to fall in love with. He would never fall for me. So why am I so conflicted? Why does my heart ache for something deeper, something more meaningful than just physical pleasure?

Maybe it's because I'm tired of being alone.

Maybe it's because I see something in him that speaks to my soul, something that goes beyond the surface-level attraction and ignites a spark deep within me.

Maybe it's also because I'm afraid of getting hurt again. I've built up walls around my cold, frozen heart to protect myself.

Maybe it's because he's different from anyone I've ever been with before. He challenges me, makes me laugh, and understands me in a way that no one does.

And maybe, just maybe, that's why I'm conflicted. Because even though I know that we can never be more than what we are right now, I can't help but imagine what it would be like to let myself believe in love again.

But reality sets in, and I know that this is just a fleeting moment in time. Our connection was never meant to last. Soon, we'll both move on to other people and other experiences.

For now, I have to enjoy the moment and focus on having the time of my life. The ocean is my best friend, and I plan to spend more time with it.

Chapter Fifteen

Kingston

I DON'T KNOW what the hell is wrong with me.

Myka isn't at all what I expected. At first glance, she seems cold and distant, but as I get closer, I experience so much of her warmth—even when she claims to be indifferent.

It's as if she's made up of both fire and ice—a combination that's both thrilling and intimidating. She's cold, but at the same time, I crave the burn that comes with being close to her.

Myka Cantú terrifies and draws me in.

There's something about her that opens me up and fills me

with more than just lust. It's a feeling that's hard to describe, but it's almost as if being with her awakens something deep within me. Perhaps it's her aura of mystery, or maybe it's her confidence and the way she handles herself.

Whatever it is, I can't deny that I'm completely drawn to her. Yep. I am completely captivated by her allure and enigmatic soul.

As I lie next to her, admiring her beauty, I realize that she has many complexities beyond what meets the eye—layers upon layers of depth within her strong spirit. Yet she appears so fragile as she sleeps in my arms.

If things were different, I could get used to waking up with Myk by my side.

"Time to wake up," I whisper, lightly brushing my lips against her ear.

Her eyes flutter open, and she looks at me with that sated gaze reserved for after we've made love. "Hi," she murmurs throatily.

"Hey," I greet her before capturing her mouth with mine. "I need you."

"I hate to break it to you," she says between kisses, "but… we're out of condoms."

"Does it matter?" I ask, looking deep into her blue, sparkly eyes.

"It should," she says. "That's an important rule for hookups."

"But we're both clean," I argue since we had this same conversation while she gave me a not-very-sexy explanation of why it's important to wear them while she gave me a blowjob a few weeks ago. "You have proof of that."

She gives me a knowing smirk. "True. Aren't you worried about babies? The pill is only ninety-nice percent effective."

I raise an eyebrow. "It sounds like they're more effective than condoms." Her smirk grows wider, and she shakes her head.

"You make some good points," she purrs, her sultry smile sending a thrill of electricity through my veins. Her hips rise to meet the rock-hard bulge beneath the sheets, and I feel my body pulled toward her like gravity. "This might just be the most enjoyable impromptu getaway I've had in ages. Great view, amazing sex... oh, and did I mention the sex?"

I don't wait for more. I thrust into her with hunger, claiming her lips with my own in an all-consuming kiss. Our tongues tangle with hunger and desire while my hands explore her curves with intimate knowledge.

When she wraps her legs around me, I slow down my movements, trying to ascertain what it is she wants from me this morning. The speed doesn't matter; all that's important is that we move together in perfect harmony. Each stroke carries us closer to blissful oblivion.

There are no walls between us now, no obstacles that can stand in our way. At this moment, I can see into the very depths of her soul, and I can feel the steady drumbeat of her heart as we make love. Something inside her is asking me to love her with a madness that can scare the bravest person alive. A desperate plea to be put together again, to be given light amidst so much darkness.

I don't understand any of that. Anyone can see that she's the light. The sunshine after a long night of stormy skies.

If I could, I would give her everything her soul seeks.

I want nothing more than to fulfill the yearning inside her, to love her with a wildness and passion that can ignite the world around us. As we lie here, intertwined in each other's arms, I know that I am the missing piece of her soul.

In this moment, I am consumed by the desire to piece her together, to give her light where there is darkness. She is my everything, and I would do anything to make her happy. There is nothing I wouldn't do for her, no sacrifice too great.

As we make love, I am filled with a sense of wonder and amazement. There is no one else in the world but us, and I am overwhelmed by the intensity of our connection. I am in awe of her, of the way she moves and the way she loves. And I know, without a doubt, that I would give her everything she could ever ask for—because that's just what you do when you love someone with all your heart and soul.

But that's the problem with me. I don't know how to love, and I don't want to put this precious woman through something that will only hurt her. As the time runs out on this vacation and reality creeps closer, the weight of the end settles in, pressing on me with a sense of emptiness and despair I've never felt.

Is this it?

Should this be the end?

Chapter Sixteen

Mr. St. James: Sorry I couldn't drive you home, but I had to be back in Seattle immediately.

Myka: Is everything okay?

Mr. St. James: Teddy was having awful nightmares. I wanted to visit her at the center and make sure she was okay.

Myka: Please don't apologize for being so amazing with her. You're a good big brother.

Mr. St. James: Did you get home alright?

Myka: Yep. Thank you for having someone stock my fridge with food and snacks.

Mr. St. James: My pleasure.

Myka: But you are aware that this goes against Rule #9, right?

Mr. St. James: Pretty sure Rule #9 pertained to my mental health—and I already got myself a counselor.

Myka: You made that up, therefore it is not applicable.

Mr. St. James: Alright, then, I don't fully agree with your Rule #9—I own a grocery chain, after all. The least I can do is to make sure you have a stocked fridge.

Myka: You're sweet, but that's not necessary.

Mr. St. James: Rule #1 of Kingston St. James decorum: Never (ever) call me sweet.

Myka: :laughing: emoji.

Mr. St. James: Don't you dare laugh at me, woman. I'm serious.

Myka: But you ARE sweet. And also kind of cute.

Mr. St. James: Enough of that or else, when we're together again, I'm gonna have to give you a spanking.

Myka: Ooh, is that a promise? :grin: emoji.

Mr. St. James: Ahh, yeah, I forgot how much you like it when I do that...

Myka: What can I say? I'm into the rough stuff.

Myka: Not always, though. You're good at knowing what I need... but let's not break Rule #12.

Mr. St. James: Which one is that?

Myka: Become Friends with Benefits with your hookup.

Mr. St. James: We're not friends... but thank fuck, there are a lot of benefits.

Mr. St. James: Are you complaining?

Myka: Nuh-uh.

Mr. St. James: So, when are you heading back up to Seattle?

Myka: There're so many projects I need to finish in the house. They need to be done before I put the house on the market.

Mr. St. James: Why don't you just hire someone to get them done?

Myka: Where's the fun in that?! Besides, I love DIY projects and I'm pretty darn good at them.

Chapter Seventeen

Myka: I want to make sure that sending groceries doesn't mean sending flowers, because that violates Rule #13.

Kingston: I don't think you ever told me, what are Rules #1 and #2?

Myka: Are you changing the topic? :raised-eyebrow: emoji.

Kingston: No, but one of us has to keep track of those rules—I don't think you'll be writing a book.

Myka: Well, so far there's just you. I'll probably have it written and edited before the next guy. :wink: emoji.

Kingston: Are you already writing me off?

Myka: I should. Probably? Rule #2: Don't sleep with the hookup more than once.

Kingston: You broke that one.

Myka: But since I haven't written the book yet, I can change it. :thinking-face: emoji.

Kingston: Amend whatever you want for the next guy, but you can't make changes to our arrangement.

Myka: Do we have an arrangement?

Kingston: I'm pretty sure there's some unwritten contract between us. We fuck while… :shrug: emoji.

Myka: Finish the sentence, St. James.

Kingston: Mr. St. James.

Myka: :laughing: emoji. You're hilarious. How's Teddy doing?

Kingston: She's revolutionizing the center and making changes. Well, her and Piper.

Myka: Piper? Right, they found her. How is she?

Kingston: All I know is that she's safe, but no one knows where she's at. So, I should assume you don't know about Archer.

Myka: What about him?

Kingston: He's alive.

Myka: I had no idea, but I'm happy for you and your family. This is what happens when I avoid my brother and his friends. I'm left out of the loop.

Kingston: It's a lot more complicated than that and shouldn't be discussed through text. He… We haven't seen him. He has amnesia and doesn't remember us.

Myka: What can I do for you?

Kingston: I'm fine.

Myka: Are you still going to therapy?

Kingston: Yes. I have two different therapists—and see them twice a week.

Myka: You should be proud of yourself.

Kingston: I am, but it's because we're opening a new location of Earth Fields Market in Canada.

Myka: There are more important things than work, but congratulations on your new branch.

Kingston: You sound like Myles.

Myka: How's good ol' Myles doing these days?

Kingston: He figured out what he wants to do next. Castles. He's going to create a whole show based on castles. I said he should try food around the world, but he said it's been done too many times.

Myka: And castles haven't?

Kingston: I wouldn't know.

Myka: He should try food. It's a lot easier.

Kingston: You're a foodie, that's why you say that.

Myka: I do like to eat. That's what you should send me next, a chef.

Kingston: Ha!

Myka: It's not funny. Send me a chef instead of food. A hot chef. ((she whispers))

Kingston: What if I promise to cook for you the next time we're together?

Myka: Have I ever told you that you're a catch?

Kingston: Am I?

Myka: Yep. You're a gentleman, you actually can cook, and sex with you is great.

Kingston: Next time I create an online profile I'll add those qualifications. Can I give your name as a reference?

Myka: You're not funny, St. James.

Kingston: I bet you laughed.

Myka: Hey, I have a yoga class in twenty. Talk to you soon?

Kingston: What happened to sexting?

Myka: Let's try it later tonight—or we could video call. I would love to watch you come all over your hand, while you're watching me do the same.

Kingston: I like how you think, minx.

Myka: TTYS

Chapter Eighteen

Myka: Do you think the buyers will say something if I leave the pool house as it is during showings?

Kingston: You have a pool house? How big is this place?

Myka: Big enough that when my family visited, I wouldn't notice they were invading my space.

Kingston: So they stayed in the pool house, and you never fixed it?

Myka: :laughing: emoji. Nope. That's my art studio, and it's messy.

Kingston: Interesting...

Myka: That doesn't answer my question.

Kingston: No, but I wonder what you do in your art studio.

Myka: Art.

Kingston: :rolling-eyes: emoji. What kind of art?

Myka: Wouldn't you want to know?

Kingston: I'm thinking… body art.

Myka: :laughing: emoji.

Myka: Let me guess, you're picturing me slathering myself in paint.

Kingston: Yes, but could we do it with some edible paint, and I'll devour you?

Myka: :thinking-face: emoji.

Myka: Nope, I won't do it.

Kingston: Oh, come on. We're always playing out your fantasies.

Myka: That's a hard limit.

Kingston: Paint, edibles, or… what?

Myka: Letting you inside my art studio.

Kingston: :raised-eyebrow: emoji.

Kingston: Tell me more...

Myka: There's nothing more to say.

Kingston: What if we do this masterpiece somewhere else in the house?

Myka: No. I'm trying to sell this place, not use it as your sex cave.

Kingston: So, if I buy the house, we can play there?

Myka: Focus, St. James.

Kingston: I have tunnel vision. All I can picture is you naked with paint all over your beautiful body. I'm willing to clean you—and dirty you up afterward.

Myka: You're not helping.

Kingston: I could help by taking you to Hawaii again. You seem stressed.

Myka: When is this trip?

Kingston: Honestly, I don't think I can take time off. Every weekend we visit Teddy, and I have to work during the week. Rain check?

Myka: I'm glad you're visiting her often.

Kingston: It's all we can do for now. Myles might ask her to work for him, since she doesn't want to go back to her old life.

Myka: Traveling around castles?

Kingston: Yes, do you think it's a good idea?

Myka: Everything is a good idea, as long as it's something she's willing to do. I'm glad you're giving her a safe space to heal—and you're supportive.

Kingston: But once she's out, we're going on vacation, right?

Myka: We'll figure that out then.

Kingston: I hate to cut this conversation short, but I have a meeting.

Myka: You should abolish meetings, they're boring.

Kingston: I try my best to make them entertaining... Next week we're having a clown, and the week after they'll come to do face painting.

Myka: Are you making fun of me?

Kingston: :wink: emoji. Talk to you soon, Myk.

Chapter Nineteen

Kingston: I'm an uncle.

Myka: Congratulations! But weren't you already an uncle? :raised-eyebrow: emoji.

Kingston: Yes. Should I say I'm an uncle for the fourth time?

Myka: Probably. Who had a baby?

Kingston: Burke. Her name is Marin, and she's the cutest little baby in the world.

Myka: I'm waiting for the picture.

Kingston: I didn't take one, but I'm sending the pic Burke texted last night. She doesn't look as cute as she is right now.

Myka: All babies are adorable, even when they're red and puffy.

Kingston: I guess, if you're a parent, you don't care much about their looks.

Myka: You'll see when you have one of those.

Kingston: My life plan doesn't include babies.

Myka: Not even one?

Kingston: Nope.

Myka: That's fair.

Kingston: How about you?

Myka: I plan on having one or two at least.

Kingston: But do you understand they are a lifetime commitment?

Myka: I do.

Kingston: Okay, then... I would offer to donate some babysitting hours to this cause, but I'm not good at taking care of babies.

Myka: As long as you don't say that when they turn 18, you'll teach them how to party, all is good with the world.

Kingston: Who would offer that?

Myka: My brother Efren. He's an idiot.

Kingston: :laughing: emoji.

Myka: It's pathetic, not funny. And as much as I would love to continue this conversation, I have to go. Dad is here.

Kingston: You got visitors.

Myka: Yes. He's helping me install a few things that require a second person.

Kingston: Have I mentioned that paying for someone might be better?

Myka: You did, but you know how I feel about it. Talk soon.

Kingston: Marin is the Antichrist.

Myka: Why would you say that?

Kingston: She's crying at all times. I think she's trying to kill the entire family. First Burke and Chloe, then it'll be the rest of the St. Jameses... be aware of the end of the world.

Myka: So you're scared of her?

Kingston: You would be, too, if you had to deal with all the crying.

Myka: Avoid her.

Kingston: I can't. I'm one of the night caregivers.

Myka: What does that entail?

Kingston: I spend the night at my brother's and take care of her, so he and Chloe can have a good night's sleep.

Myka: :laughing: emoji.

Myka: :laughing: emoji.

Myka: :laughing: emoji.

Myka: :laughing: emoji.

Myka: :laughing: emoji.

Kingston: Stop laughing at me.

Myka: I wish I could, but this is too precious. You, the guy who's allergic to children—and is afraid of them, too—is babysitting his niece.

Kingston: I am, along with many other volunteers. Though I wouldn't call ourselves volunteers when Mrs. Bradley technically forced us to agree to this crazy plan.

Myka: She's scarier than her badass, super-agent husband. And though I want to stick around and see if Marin destroys you tonight, I have to sleep.

Kingston: Are you abandoning me in my time of need?

Myka: You'll be fine. :wink-tongue: emoji.

Myka: Did you survive the weekend with your niece?

Kingston: I did. As a thank-you for not bailing on them, Chloe made me breakfast.

Myka: I'm glad things worked out. I'm guessing Marin isn't the Antichrist, and you're all going to be fine?

Kingston: Hopefully. How's the house going?

Myka: It's almost done.

Kingston: You never told me what you decided to do with the art studio.

Myka: I left it the way it was... They made me convert my beautiful house into some model home. I couldn't give up the last piece of my soul just because I need to sell this house.

Kingston: Do you have to sell it?

Myka: It makes more sense.

Kingston: Are you moving back to Seattle?

Myka: Once it's sold.

Kingston: Looking forward to seeing you again.

Myka: Who said we're going back to hooking up? That's a little presumptuous of you.

Kingston: Is this because I haven't visited you?

Myka: No, I'm not saying that.

Kingston: I could go down there, you know.

Myka: What's going on with Teddy?

Kingston: She's somewhere in Europe, working for Myles and hanging out with Archer's new dad.

Myka: You mean Finnegan's dad.

Kingston: Not you, too.

Myka: Listen, I had a long conversation with Manelik about this. It was hard to convince Lang that he has to accept Archer's identity as Finnegan—that Finnegan's a person. But even Lang's managed to accept it.

Kingston: He's Archer, my little brother.

Myka: No, he's Finnegan, a man who's suffered a tragedy and who's trying to adjust to a new life. Be patient and loving.

Kingston: You sound like my counselor.

Myka: Sorry for your loss, but you should consider this as an opportunity to make a new friend—and sometimes friends can become your family.

Kingston: I can try that.

Myka: Hey, the realtor is here. I have to sign the documents so this house goes into the MLS listing and sells ASAP.

Kingston: Good luck. :shamrock: emoji.

Chapter Twenty

Kingston

WHAT AM I DOING HERE?

As I stand outside Myka's house, my eyes are drawn to its stucco exterior in a creamy shade of white that seems to glow in the warm California sun. The red-tiled roof stands out boldly against the bright blue sky, and I can see the ocean sparkling in the distance.

I take a few steps closer and admire the ornate wrought-iron railings along the balcony on the second floor, complete with decorative shutters on each window, lending a touch of elegance to an otherwise plain façade.

The garden is a verdant paradise of succulents, palm trees, and other tropical plants, thriving in the dry climate. The colors and textures weave together into a natural oasis that contrasts with the urban surroundings. This place reflects Myka's personality.

"I don't get why she wants to sell it," I mutter out loud, mesmerized as I take in the house.

As I continue to gaze at the house, I can't help but imagine myself living here. Lounging on the deck, maybe sipping an ice-cold drink while watching the sunset over the ocean. Or entertaining guests in an outdoor kitchen while my kids splash around in the pool.

Does it have an outdoor kitchen? If not, I could hire someone to design something that'll blend with the pool and the backyard atmosphere.

I blink a couple of times, startled by my thoughts. Where the fuck did that come from?

"Snap out of the trance, St. James," I scold myself. Must be a side effect from going to therapy and sleepless nights watching Marin—or the few times I watched over Zach's children.

Since when does Kingston St. James imagine a future that involves more than just work and the flavor of the day? What's next? Checking the best school districts in the country for the kids he should never have? And why the fuck am I talking to myself, and in third person?

Therapy isn't doing shit. I blame Myles and his terrible advice.

"It's what Teddy needs from us," Myles said. "Not just Teddy, but all of us—so we can move on from the trauma we dealt with growing up."

He went on about how our parents had "screwed us up" with their marriage and nasty divorce. Then there's Archer, our younger brother, and his mysterious disappearance and miraculous reappearance.

I run a hand through my hair and sigh.

Piper was right. He's alive. Archer wasn't dead. Apparently, he had been injured during his mission and has amnesia. My beloved brother forgot all about our family, and he doesn't want to be a part of us anymore—what am I supposed to do with that?

Not run to Myka Cantú the first chance you get out of the office.

I should've started a new profile on WildMatch and found someone else to hook up with for the weekend. Instead, I jumped on my private jet and came to see her.

It has been a few months since the last time we saw each other. I should've called and checked if she still lived here—or if she had sold the house. When I ring the bell, a middle-aged man in a well-fitted suit opens the door and says, "You must be Raymond Stewart," extending his hand with a bright smile. "It's nice to finally put a face to the voice. I'm thrilled to show you your new house."

He exudes a confident and professional demeanor as he introduces himself as the real estate agent.

"Kingston St. James," I correct him, clasping his hand as a wave of disappointment crashes over me at Myka's absence.

"Do you have an appointment to see the place?" He casts an appraising glance at me and then he looks at the property.

"No. I don't have an appointment," I reply, trying to decide whether I should call Myka or wait for her to show up. This impromptu visit is an utter fiasco—maybe I should head back home.

"It's fine. I can show it to you while I wait for Mr. Stewart…" He trails off, eyeing me curiously. "Unless you already have an agent?"

"No agent," I say, instead of mentioning that I'm here to visit the owner.

"Marcus Reid." He gives me a card and opens the door wide so I can follow him. "Welcome to your future home, Mr. St. James."

That's unlikely to happen. I live in Seattle, close to my family. They need me there. Moving isn't an option.

"This is the perfect place for a big family," Marcus says, waving a hand so I'll follow him. "The master bedroom is like an entire apartment away from the rest of the house. How many children do you have?"

"No children," I answer, staring at the empty gray walls. This doesn't look anything like the house Myka owns in Luna Harbor, or the apartment she rents in Seattle.

"Welcome to your future home," he repeats for maybe the third or fourth time.

Does he think that telling me a gazillion times that this is my piece of property will make me sign? It takes a lot more than that.

I scowl at him, but he doesn't care. He continues with the

tour. "This is one of the most luxurious homes in La Jolla. As you can see, it features stunning ocean views, a state-of-the-art home theater, and a breathtaking infinity pool."

"Wow," I breathe out as we step into the grand foyer, marveling at the opulence of my surroundings—the marble floors, modern chandeliers, sleek furniture—all of it managing to feel cozy, despite its grandeur.

Marcus grins at my reaction and leads me around the house. His enthusiasm is contagious as he goes on and on about its features. "The kitchen is a chef's dream, with top-of-the-line appliances and a massive island."

"Even I would want to cook in here," I mutter, trying to play along and keeping my annoyance at bay—but I'm doing a shitty job.

"Wait until you see the master bedroom," he says, a smirk on his face and a glint in his eyes.

This poor bastard swears I'm going to buy the place. He couldn't be more wrong. I should tell him why I'm here, instead of going through Myka's house without her consent.

"Do you like big bedrooms?" Marcus asks as I continue following him.

"Who doesn't?" I answer, overwhelmed by the amount of space and his chatter.

"Well, you'll love this one. The room is fit for royalty, with a fireplace, a private balcony, and a spa-like bathroom." He pauses, smirking. "You and the missus can enjoy the space without having to worry about any guests or your future children."

"No kids," I insist, feeling defensive. I'm not sure if I'm

telling him, or if I'm trying to convince myself that children aren't part of my future.

The bedroom is like an apartment isolated from the rest of the house. It's inviting, and when I spot the terrace, I smirk. It's easy to picture bending Myka there to fuck her hard under the moonlight.

Fuck, where did that come from?

I'm horny? The last time I had sex was... Hawaii? I shouldn't care, though. It was a hookup, and... I should probably excuse myself and leave the house. I need to find someone else to have sex with. That'll snap me out of this stupid trance.

"Shall we continue?" Marcus looks at me expectantly.

We walk in and out of six bedrooms that can be converted into offices or guest rooms. Though, there's a big home office, too. When we step outside, I can't help but gasp at the view. The infinity pool seems to spill right into the ocean, and the sound of waves crashing against the shore is like music to my ears. I can picture a couple of children splashing in the pool. A strange tug in my gut begs me to run away.

There's still time to leave and never look back, but I don't. I'm trying to figure out where I'll set the outdoor kitchen. Marcus drags me out of my trance by saying, "Hey, want to check out the pool house? It has a kitchen and might need some remodeling. But it's perfect for when the in-laws visit."

"Why does it need to be remodeled?" I inquire, intrigued.

"It's currently an art studio," he reveals. "You'll need new appliances and counters. It might take some scrubbing to get rid of all that paint on the floor, but..."

I frown, not liking the idea of transforming Myka's studio.

If anyone buys it, they'll destroy her space. I can't allow that to happen. It's her sanctuary. Actually, I have to stop the showings to keep people from entering her space.

"Is this house under contract yet?" I interrupt with an uncharacteristic eagerness.

Marcus shakes his head. "Not that I'm aware. There's been some interest, but no offers… yet." He presses his lips together. "The asking price is high, and the owner is not willing to compromise."

I nod determinedly. "Listen, I need to make some calls, but you'll hear from my people in no time."

Marcus raises his eyebrows in disbelief. "That fast?"

"Yes," I say determinedly, already reaching for my phone.

I reach out to my lawyer, who promises to start the transaction as soon as possible. Since it'll be handled with cash and with one of my companies, he doesn't think it's going to take long.

I ask him to keep my identity a secret. Myka doesn't need to know that, a few weeks shy from my thirty-ninth birthday, I must be in the middle of an identity crisis or… what the fuck is wrong with me?

If anything, I can sell this house in a couple of years for a profit. Isn't that what matters? The bottom line.

Chapter Twenty-One

Myka

MY HEART IS POUNDING in my chest as I park the car. There's a lot I have to figure out within the next couple of hours.

The call—it changed everything. I thought I was ready, but...

It feels as if I've waited an eternity for it, and now here I am, overwhelmed with fear and anticipation.

The mother-to-be wants an in-person interview with me, so she can make a decision. My future teeters on her judgment. Joy mixed with apprehension.

What if she writes me off for being single? What if she doesn't think I'm fit to raise these babies?

Two of them.

She's expecting two babies.

This would be the perfect beginning to our little family—but she might not give me a glance.

From what I gathered, the only reason she's calling me is because I'm willing to take them both—and I have twin experience. I snort at that logic. Just because I am one, it doesn't mean I know how to raise twins.

Can I truly raise two babies on my own?

The weighty responsibility burns heavily within me. These babies, who require someone to love and care for them, will depend on me—can I provide what they need?

Will I be enough?

The doubts swirl around me like a dark cloud, threatening to swallow me whole.

The past shouldn't matter. This is the call I've been waiting for all along. I'm ready for them. I have so much love to give, and so much to offer. And even if she doesn't choose me, I have to try.

I just need to figure out a way to make it to Portland by tomorrow—without having to call in any favors. I don't want my family to learn about this just yet.

When I approach my house, my stomach drops at the sight of Kingston St. James standing at the entrance. It's been so long since the last time we were together.

Hawaii was too many minutes and miles ago. He shouldn't be here. Not today. It's not that I don't like him or that I don't want to see him. It's that... I have too many things going on at once to entertain him.

"You should have called," I say coldly, instead of greeting him. I immediately regret my tone. It's not his fault that my mind is too preoccupied with so many things.

He steps closer and takes off my sunglasses. "Hello to you too," he says with a smirk as he leans in and kisses my cheek softly. "What happened?"

I blink a couple of times, trying to understand his question. "Why are you upset?" he responds to my silence.

I sigh. "It's..." I trail off and close my mouth, knowing he's not going to care, and I don't want him involved.

"Take a deep breath, and let's try to talk this over," he murmurs in an unusually calm and understanding voice.

I unlock the door with my phone, and we slip inside, my mind already spinning with worries. "There are two people interested in the house. One of them is going to send an offer soon," I tell him, my nose scrunching at the unwelcome thought of selling it.

Kingston looks at me questioningly. "And you don't want to sell it?"

I sigh heavily and scrunch up my nose again. "I have to."

He tilts his head toward the door. "Yes, but you're telling me that you don't want to sell it?"

I exhale heavily. "I'm not sure, but I have to do it. It makes more sense for me to move to Seattle with my family, but this place..." I trail off, gesturing at the warm air and the beachfront outside my window. "It will be hard to leave it behind.

Especially when—" I clamp my mouth shut. He doesn't need to know about the adoption.

"Go on," he encourages.

"That's the part that frustrates me most," I confess, biting my lip. "I got a call, and I need to be in Portland tomorrow. That's a seventeen-hour drive."

"Why can't you fly?"

"I couldn't find any flights, and calling my brothers for help isn't an option," I say, hoping that he doesn't suggest I call his cousin. If I do, Manelik will hear about it, and I don't want my family involved. Not until I know for sure these little ones will be mine.

He holds up his phone. "I got this," he says. "Pack your things. We'll be there in a couple of hours."

My brows pinch together in surprise. "What?"

"I can get us there right now," he says confidently, already dialing a number on his phone.

Any other day I'd turn him down, but I'm desperate to arrive in Oregon and wasn't looking forward to a long drive. "Are you sure you can take me there?" I ask as I open the door and make my way inside the house.

He nods wordlessly. "While we're in the air," he says softly, "you can tell me more about your seller's remorse." He smirks teasingly at me before continuing his call, and I have to chuckle despite myself.

I stifle a laugh and, once he's done barking orders, I say, "That's not a thing."

He quirks an eyebrow and his mouth lifts slightly at one

corner. "It sounds like it is." His voice is gentle as he adds, "Are you feeling okay?"

"Why do you ask?" I reply lightly, arching my own eyebrow in challenge.

He shrugs a shoulder almost dismissively as he taps away on his phone, muttering something about the pilot and making sure the jet is ready. "You usually plan better than this. How long do we need to stay there?"

"I got the call less than an hour ago," I respond and then add, "You're going to laugh when I say, 'I didn't ask.' But I suppose not more than a couple of days."

His gaze narrows as he sizes me up, scrutinizing my face and body language. "You look frazzled. What else is going on? I'm sure the sale of the house isn't what has you tied up in knots."

I gulp, trying to dislodge the lump that has taken residence in my throat. "The mother of my future children wants to see me in person. What if she realizes I'm unfit to care for them?"

His eyes are fixed on me, and his expression is unreadable for what feels like an eternity. My heart gallops in my chest as I wait, unsure of what he's thinking. Finally, he breaks the silence with one word: "Children?"

I nod.

"You're adopting a child?" His tone turns cold and distant. "Why didn't I know that?"

"I haven't mentioned it to anyone." I pause and shrug before I say, "You know, trying not to jinx it and all that. Everyone expects me to do everything the traditional way. Find the guy, fall in love, and… That's definitely not for me."

He stares at me for a moment, the silence between us growing heavy. I can see the way he wants to run away. "Wow. You're going to be a mom."

The words hang in the air, and I can practically feel my heart breaking, slowing down. Kingston suddenly seems so cold, so distant—it's like he's already written me off as an unfit mother-to-be. Or maybe he's afraid I'll stick him with the responsibility.

Yep, he's backing away, mentally and emotionally, readying himself to flee after dropping me at the airport. I don't care if he doesn't approve, or if this is the last time I see him. He's just proving my point. I made the right decision by doing this on my own.

"A mom," he mutters one more time.

"Maybe. We'll see after this interview—if it goes well. Let me know if you can't take me there, and I'll figure something else out. It's all good."

I pivot on my heel and march away without even glancing over my shoulder at him. And without hesitation or doubt that this is what's best for me. This is exactly why I don't get attached to people. They always leave.

Chapter Twenty-Two

Myka

I SWALLOW hard and force a smile considering how we left things at my house. "This is very nice of you," I say, glancing around the airplane's cabin, my stomach churning. Is this trip even worth it?

King cocks his head and smirks. "Are we going to start with pleasantries?"

"What do you mean?" I ask, confusion knitting my brow.

"You're trying to fill the silence," he responds. "That's not like you."

I snort, shaking my head. "No offense, but you don't know me that well. If you did, you'd know I'm about to puke from all the knots in my stomach."

"Afraid of flying?" he inquires.

"No, of rejection," I whisper, my voice wavering slightly as I take a seat.

"Just remember, they'll be lucky to have you," he says, squeezing my hand reassuringly.

I scoff, dusting off my leggings and fidgeting with the hem of my top. I've never been this nervous in my entire life. "Doubtful. I'm her last resort—the shelter is working on other solutions…" I trail off for a moment before continuing with a heavy sigh.

"What does that mean?" His voice is soft, soothing like a balm as he moves closer and takes my hand in his. I can feel the warmth radiating from his touch, the sincerity in his gaze, the compassion in his words.

What is wrong with this picture? This isn't how the notorious playboy Kingston St. James behaves. He's supposed to be charismatic, charming, but also afraid of making any deep connections. I need him distant and cold like he was at my house—void of feelings—which I can handle just fine.

Why is he all of a sudden trying to be understanding and supportive? Why is he acting like one of those men who will do anything for the woman they love?

He doesn't love me. He doesn't even know me, not really—not the depths of my soul, the secrets I keep hidden, the darkness I carry. And I don't need this—him or his kindness. Not when I'm in the middle of an existential crisis.

I'm stuck in between thoughts, searching for what comes next and if it's worth the effort to put myself out. The weight of it all is crushing me, suffocating me, and he's trying… What is he trying to do?

It's on the tip of my tongue to tell him that I don't want his help. I don't need his kindness. I prefer to be left alone—to figure it out on my own.

But do I want to drown in the darkness of my thoughts?

A thousand conflicting feelings, ideas, and memories battle for power inside my mind. While one part of me wants to shove him away and prove that I'm strong enough to figure this out on my own, the other yearns for his warmth and safety.

That part craves his embrace like a lifeline of safety in a raging storm.

I don't know what to do, how to feel.

I'm lost, adrift in a sea of emotions.

For now, I'll let him hold my hand. For now, I'll let him be kind. Tomorrow, we'll go our separate ways and never talk again.

As I struggle with this internal debate, he looks at me with an inquisitive expression and asks, "Myk?"

My throat tightens as I take a steadying breath and begin my story. "She—the biological mom—wanted a couple to adopt her child. She found the perfect couple, but Mr. and Mrs. Perfect only wanted one kid. Once they found out she was having twins, they backed out." His gaze remains steady, waiting for me to continue.

I pull a few strands of hair and fidget with them as I become more anxious with every passing second. "It's been a couple of months, and no one is good enough for her babies," I say, desperation edging into my voice. "I get it. You want the best for your children. But she doesn't have much time and is getting desperate. Thea Decker suggested me—since I have the financial stability."

His expression is inquisitive as he looks at me, waiting for my response. "But that's not enough?"

I shake my head. "Nope. She agreed to interview me. Apparently, she liked that I have experience with twins, but she has her doubts. I would be a single mother." I press my lips together and then release a hysterical laugh. "Why am I even bothering to go and meet her?"

Kingston doesn't respond. Instead, he pulls me into an embrace the best he could while we're seated, and just sways me in silence. I appreciate the comfort he offers without words. As the plane takes off, I relax into his arms, letting out a deep sigh when the pilot announces we're at a high altitude.

"Have you applied to any other adoption agencies?" he asks, right before the flight attendant appears.

"Would you like anything to drink?" she purrs, looking only at Kingston with an inviting smile.

"Tequila, chilled," I say, then add, "And a glass of water, please."

"For you, *sir*?" She slowly shifts her gaze at him like prey eyeing its predator. She really wants him, doesn't she?

"A glass of Macallan on the rocks, please," he says calmly in return, ignoring her alluring behavior.

The flight attendant gives him another sultry smile. "Anything to eat, sir?"

He turns away from her gaze with a barely concealed roll of his eyes before responding. "Myk?"

I shake my head, amused by the flight attendant's behavior. "I'm not hungry, but if you want to order anything…" I trail off, unsure how to tell him that if he needs to entertain this woman, I'm fine with it.

"We're good, thank you," he answers her dismissively and turns back to me with a mischievous grin on his face.

I raise an eyebrow in surprise, then glance at him again expectantly. "Have you two…?"

"Please finish that sentence," he says, almost laughing as he shakes his head in astonishment at my boldness.

"She was offering herself as a meal," I reply cheekily.

He snorts with laughter. "Is that a problem?"

Smiling, I shake my head. "Nope. I was going to say, 'Don't mind me. Go and do your thing.'"

He pauses and grins appreciatively. "This is what I like about you. You don't filter yourself and you call me out on my bullshit." Lifting his eyebrows, he prods further. "Just so you know, I've never seen her before, and I'm not interested in her."

He takes a breath and then adds seriously, "Since we're being honest, why are you regretting the sale of the house?"

"You're going to think I'm crazy, but as I took the decorations down and added one boring touch after another, so it would appeal to potential buyers, I questioned my decision." Pausing for a moment, I recall the exact moment my phone rang, and I saw the shelter's name on the screen. "Then the call came, and when they told me they were twins, I thought this house would be perfect for them."

Kingston nods. "It's a big place," he says, finishing my sentence. "The pool is ideal for kids."

"Yeah," I agree. "But…"

"Do you see yourself loving someone else's child?" he inquires.

I nod, thinking of Rumi—the little girl we welcomed into our family with no questions asked. She has parents, but she'll always be part of the Cantú family. I mention her and all the babies that have been around Luna Harbor.

"I remember Iskander's niece," he says and doesn't wait for me to answer. "I saw her at Iskander and Siobhan's place the other day."

I feel a twinge of envy at his words, because I miss the little tyke. I shouldn't be upset. I'm the one who chose to stay away from Seattle while dealing with the renos of my house. Shaking off the negativity, I ask, "Isn't she adorable?"

"She's a beauty," he agrees. "But you have to remember that, once you become a mother, it'll be hard for you to find a partner. Don't you worry about it?"

"I don't want a partner—or to fall in love," I reply, my voice calm and matter-of-fact.

Kingston doesn't look at me like I'm crazy for not following social norms. Instead, he just nods as if he understands.

"Society expects us to follow their arbitrary rules," I continue, passion rising within me. "College, a nine-to-five job, marriage… People expect you to do as they say, without caring if it brings you happiness." My chest rises and falls as I take a deep breath, finishing my rant.

"You're right. Life is not a grocery list," Kingston replies sagely. His words echo in my head, and I know instinctively he's right: life should be lived on our own terms, not according to someone else's expectations.

In that short sentence, he seems to understand me better than anyone else has in years. He sees right through me and knows exactly who I am. I'm relieved to know that someone accepts my unconventional choices without judgment or forcing me into predetermined boxes society deems appropriate.

Kingston understands me without question and without bias toward what society expects from me. Maybe having him as a friend while I figure out my future wouldn't be such a bad thing after all.

He takes off his seat belt and helps me with mine. "Come on, I know what's going to make you relax," he says, taking my mouth.

As his lips press against mine, a wave of electricity shoots through my body, causing me to gasp in surprise. I can feel the intensity of his desire in the way he holds me, his arms pulling me closer, his fingers tangling in my hair. I should pull away, but my heart is pounding so hard I can barely think straight.

All I can focus on is the heat of his lips against mine, the way his tongue flicks against my bottom lip, urging me to open up to him. My hands reach up to grab on to his shoulders, pulling him even closer.

But then, as quickly as it began, he pulls away, leaving me breathless and wanting more. We make our way toward the private room. As we stare into each other's eyes, I can feel the uncertainty of this moment. *Maybe this isn't such a good idea after all*, I think to myself, my heart racing with conflicting emotions.

But then, as he leans in to kiss me again, I realize that I don't care. In this moment, nothing else matters except the intense passion that we share.

It's just a moment. A way to forget my current struggles. Tomorrow I'll let him go and we'll never see each other again.

Chapter Twenty-Three

Kingston

WHEN WE TOUCH down in Portland, Myka rapidly texts Thea Decker to let her know we're here. She isn't surprised when they switch the meeting for today and ask us to be there within the next couple of hours.

I drive us to the Merkel Hotel—where my assistant has booked our stay for the next few days. Myka wants to clean up and change into something more appropriate for her interview with the mother-to-be. She's too wound up. I plan to help her relieve some of that stress with food and a quick fuck before we leave.

Myk only agrees to a quick shower—and a couple of orgasms. We leave the hotel as soon as we're ready and arrive at our destination with five minutes to spare.

"You're efficient," she remarks as I open the car door for her, extending my hand to help her out of the vehicle.

I flash a playful wink. "Always."

She turns her attention to her jeans and conservative sweater. "Do I look okay?"

"You look fine," I reply calmly, but not meeting her gaze.

"Just fine?" she inquires with a note of disappointment in her voice.

Gently, I place my hand on her shoulder and meet her gaze firmly. "Babe, you always look spectacular. Right now, you're trying too hard to be someone you're not. Currently, your clothes scream 'J. Crew catalog circa 2000.'"

Myka glares at me, but I remain undeterred. "If you want to ace this interview, you have to show her who you truly are and what kind of person her kids would get as a mom."

"What if she doesn't like me?" Myka worries aloud.

Her concern is valid, but I'm not sure what to answer. Thankfully, a couple approaches us from farther down the sidewalk. Without any difficulty, I recognize Thea Decker and her husband, Tristan, who strides right beside her. Thea's violet, expressive eyes remind me so much of Piper's. Maybe later I can ask her about my former sister-in-law. She could be the key to getting Archer back into the St. James family.

Myka waves at them, mouthing a hello.

"Hello, Thea, Tristan," I greet them.

"Myka, Kingston," Tristan says curtly with a nod.

Thea hugs us both warmly before saying, "Glad you were able to make it. You look a little nervous, sweetheart—is everything okay?"

"I don't handle rejection well," Myka admits, her voice small.

Thea gives Myka a motherly smile and cups her face affectionately. "Rejection is hard. I understand you're scared, but let me paint you a different picture. There's a pregnant, sixteen-year-old girl who was rejected by her boyfriend. Kicked out of her house by her parents, and… well, you know what happened to the first couple she chose."

She pauses, looking at both of us. "Can you imagine how she feels? We do our best to support her, but we're not enough —and what if she makes the wrong decision?"

Myka's face contorts in realization, and she mumbles softly, "She needs support and understanding."

Thea tenderly squeezes Myka's hand and nods reassuringly. "Exactly. Do you think you can give it to her, no matter the outcome?"

Myka confidently smiles back at Thea and replies, "Of course—even if she decides to take a different route or finds someone better."

Thea gives Myka an approving squeeze on the hand. "I knew you'd understand," she remarks kindly as she beckons us to follow her into the building.

Truth be told, I don't quite understand the full magnitude of their conversation. However, I remain quiet and follow them as they make their way toward the shelter—or what looks like an apartment building.

Before entering the interview room, we learn that Shiloh Griffin turns seventeen in three months and her due date is in approximately eight weeks. And I learn that twins sometimes arrive earlier. She is currently a junior in high school and plans to go back to school.

Though I should wait outside the apartment, I can't seem to let go of Myka. Even courageous people need a rock to lean on during tough moments—and that is precisely why I'm here, holding Myka's hand as we prepare for this daunting interview.

As the CEO of one of the fastest-growing companies in the world, I can safely say that I'm an interview expert.

I've interviewed hundreds of candidates for several key positions, but nothing can be compared to this. I can't compare those times to what happened just now. There weren't many questions, but Myka gave her all the tips on how to choose the right parents for the twins.

Not only that, but Myka offered to help Shiloh, emotionally and financially, if she's not sure about giving the babies up for adoption. She offered to pay for the trip to Seattle to check out the shelter Thea Decker runs for single mothers. And to sponsor her—whatever that means. That's the kind of woman I've fallen in love with.

. . .

"You do know that you technically forfeited the children, right?" I ask as we make our way out of the conference room.

Myka smiles sadly. "They aren't a trophy or part of some game," she says softly. "I don't think Shiloh is ready to let them go. In fact, I'm pretty sure she's giving them up out of desperation."

"But what about you?" I press, concerned because this is part of her dream, isn't it?

She shrugs indifferently. "If not her, someone else will pick me."

Thea and Tristan are waiting in the hallway. Glancing at Myka's hopeful expression, I say, "Give me a second. I think I left my phone on the table."

Rushing back into the room, I find a few girls with Shiloh, discussing her options. "Did you forget something?" one of them asks curiously.

"No," I say solemnly, handing Shiloh my business card. "But listen, if you need anything, call me—and if you decide to give the babies up for adoption, keep Myka in mind. She would be the best mother for your children."

Shiloh examines the card closely while looking at me with a glimmer of hope in her eyes. She weakly protests, "Yeah… but she will only be one parent. I want them to have a good family."

"Myka isn't alone. She has all the love in the world, and your children will be lucky to have her. Also, she has an extraordinary family who embraces everyone that gets near or becomes a part of it—so much so that everybody feels loved and accepted without any judgment whatsoever. Your children will not only have the most amazing mother in the world, they'll have plenty of uncles, aunties, and cousins they can turn to whenever they need anything," I say, turning around.

One of the girls asks, her voice small and meek, "But are you sure she would want more than just one baby?"

I slowly look back over my shoulder, but find them all hidden in the shadows of the room. Swiveling back around, I smile knowingly. "She will," I assure them, flashing a grin. "And as a bonus, she has twin experience."

Shiloh's eyes fill with moisture. I swallow hard and leave the place. My heart weighs heavy with emotion as I step outside. Shiloh's situation is heartbreaking, and Myka's feelings and dreams intertwined with it only make it worse. It feels right for Myka to be a mother to Shiloh's children, but the decision isn't mine to make.

Why am I even getting myself involved? I know that the best thing to do is walk away. I have my own problems—and a family to deal with.

Just walk away, St. James. This isn't your circus.

Chapter Twenty-Four

Kingston: Any news about the babies?

Myka: She's going to keep them.

Kingston: Are you okay?

Myka: Of course. I think it's the best for her babies.

Kingston: I need to know if you're okay.

Myka: You're worrying too much about a hookup.

Kingston: I'm afraid to tell you that we've moved from hookup to friends with benefits.

Myka: What are these benefits?

Kingston: There are plenty: unlimited sex, a person to lean on, and daily food deliveries.

Myka: You don't need to deliver me food, but I appreciate you. And do you realize that if I accept this new arrangement, I have to create new rules?

Kingston: :facepalm: emoji.

Kingston: Forget I said anything.

Myka: But the rules are so much fun.

Kingston: Sure, but we always end up breaking them. When are you coming back to Seattle?

Myka: Next week.

Kingston: Why not this week?

Myka: I'm packing my things. A company bought my house, and they'll probably do something stupid with it. Thankfully, they gave me enough time to move out. I can pack my art studio slowly.

Myka: You know what's weird about this transaction?

Kingston: What?

Myka: They said that if I ever want it back, I can have it—they'll refund my money.

Kingston: Why is that weird?

Myka: No one does that willingly. I'm guessing that they're using it for a movie set, and once they're done, they won't have use for it.

Kingston: Wouldn't they rent it instead?

Myka: You might be right. I have no idea why they bought it.

Kingston: Is anyone helping you pack?

Myka: Nope. I don't want my family to learn that I'm about to move back to Seattle.

Kingston: Are you planning a vacation?

Myka: I'm still debating.

Kingston: Will you invite me?

Myka: We'll see.

Kingston: Hey, Mom is in my office. Can I text you later?

Myka: Yep.

Kingston: If I had time, I would go to visit you.

Myka: What's happening?

Kingston: Mom came, then Dad joined. They fought in my office—and I regressed thirty years.

Myka: This would be a good time to call one of your therapists.

Kingston: It's easier if I sex it out instead of talking it out.

Myka: :laughing: emoji.

Myka: Wait, let me write down your nonsense.

Kingston: Why?

Myka: It's priceless, and if you end up breaking your "I'm never getting married" plan, I can give them to your future bride.

Kingston: :big-frown: emoji.

Kingston: :fearful: emoji.

Kingston: :anxious-with-sweat: emoji.

Kingston: You wouldn't dare to do that. Rule #1 of our FWB arrangement: We shall not use our text messages against the other.

Myka: Fine, I won't. As long as you go to the therapist and work out your regression after your parents fought in your office.

Kingston: I didn't say that, but are you blackmailing me, Cantú?

Myka: It's logical. And no. I'm just trying to help you become a better version of Kingston St. James.

Kingston: I will do it under one condition.

Myka: Nope. You have to get help because you want to help yourself. :wink: emoji.

Kingston: Let me think about it. But please tell me when you're back in Seattle.

Myka: I'll try.

Kingston: I heard you're in Seattle.

Myka: You people are worse than a small town.

Kingston: I'm coming to your place.

Myka: Actually, I arrived last night and left this morning for Luna Harbor. This is exactly why I didn't call you. I stayed at Manelik's, and we left at four in the morning.

Kingston: Why would you do that?

Myka: It's Grandpa's birthday this weekend, and we wanted to start the celebrations today.

Kingston: Oh, right. I did receive an invite to a party Saturday night.

Myka: Are you coming?

Kingston: No. I'm going to be in New York with Myles. Archer is there, and we're trying to figure out a way to get close to him.

Myka: I hope things work out for you.

Kingston: We're not sure if they will. He didn't recognize Piper, and she finally let him go. After eight years, she let him go.

Myka: How do you know?

Kingston: She came to my office, trying to figure out how to give back everything she received from Archer throughout their time together.

Kingston: It's like she's divorcing him, but without signing anything, because, thanks to my mother, he's legally dead.

Myka: What do you mean?

Kingston: She changed his status from MIA to dead.

Myka: But he's back. Does she know?

Kingston: She did it before we learned he's back, and no, she doesn't know.

Kingston: We don't want to tell her until he's willing to see her. I don't want to break her heart.

Myka: I hope things get better.

Kingston: When will I see you?

Myka: I should be back in Seattle next week, but soon I have to go to Portland. I have to be around for Shiloh.

Kingston: You're going to help her with the babies?

Myka: Yes. I'm her coach.

Kingston: You're a good person, Myka Cantú. Call me if you need me.

Myka: Same.

Chapter Twenty-Five

Kingston

"Is everything alright?" I ask, my voice heavy with concern as Lang steps back into the conference room he left twenty minutes ago without a word.

He waves a hand dismissively, adjusting his suit with a smooth flick of his fingers. "All is fine," he assures me. "Why don't you go back to signing the documents?"

Fitz arches an eyebrow, leaning forward in his chair. "Are you sure it's okay? You locked us in and set the security to panic room mode."

My mouth drops open in disbelief. "Is that what happened? All those bolts and noises were you locking us in the room?" I whistle low. "Should I remind you that I just came here to finish the purchase of Healthy for You stores? I mean… what's next?"

Fitz shakes his head, an exasperated smile on his lips. "Nothing is going to happen. It's just another day at the office. You get used to his overreactions."

"Well, at least tell us what happened," I insist, crossing my arms over my chest.

Lang sighs heavily, resignation clouding his features. "It was your brother, demanding to see Fitz—claiming he had a major emergency." His words hang in the air while they each exchange meaningful glances before he adds, "The receptionist didn't know he's harmless, so she activated the emergency alarm."

I lean back in my chair, one eyebrow raised skeptically. "Which one, Fletcher? Did he get fired from the Orcas and needs Fitz to sue them?"

A soft snort escapes him as Lang presses his lips together tightly before saying, "Finnegan Gil—the St. James brother formerly known as Archer."

My eyes widen in surprise as understanding slowly dawns on me. "He was here?" I whisper incredulously.

Lang nods once and meets my gaze steadily. "Yep. I think he finally realized who Piper is to him—and that she dropped him like a hot coal."

"Ah." I don't know what else to add. I'm still baffled that, after waiting for so long, she decided to give up on him. "He invited us to have dinner with him tonight," I say, gulping down my apprehension about whether he'll cancel on us. Is he going to cancel on us?

"Well, if he cancels, you guys can come to ours," Lang offers, a twinkle in his eye. "I'll cook."

"So why did he come again?" I query, curiosity sparking in me.

Lang smirks with satisfaction. "He's losing his shit because Piper returned everything he gifted her and he wanted to give everything back to her and to make things better."

I furrow my brows, confused at why Lang seems so pleased about it. "Is that a good thing?"

"Not in the short term," Lang admits. "The poor asshole looks like an abandoned puppy. He lost his Piper. The man can't remember anything, but his heart knows what that means. My guess is that he's about to learn who he was and, hopefully, he'll accept us back into his life."

My phone buzzes with a text from Myles, telling me Finnegan has had a family emergency and canceled our dinner plans.

"Are you sure we can join you?" I ask before I reply to my brother that we're still on for dinner.

"Of course. My man will cook for you," Fitz offers, winking at Lang. It only takes that little gesture for my cousin to lean closer and start kissing him. I sigh, annoyed, and message Myles on the change of plans—we'll be having dinner at Lang's instead of going home.

I clear my throat to get their attention. "Are you two done?"

Lang pulls away from Fitz, glancing at me with a mischievous grin. "You're just bitter because there's no one to go back home to," he teases. "What happened with Myka Cantú? Didn't you guys have a thing?"

Fitz stares at him blankly, and Lang recaps what he knows about me and Myka.

"We were just having fun," I say, my voice laced with a defensive edge.

Lang's smirk widens as he drums his fingers on the desk. "Sure… how's the new house in San Diego? You paid almost double the asking price. That, my friend, is called love."

I groan in response. "It's not love. And we're not friends, we're cousins."

He gives me a look that says, it's all the same.

I glower at him and say, "And using my personal transactions to tease the fuck out of me should be illegal—or unethical." My tone is sharp and accusing. "You're fired. I'll start searching for a better lawyer—one who doesn't gossip."

Lang chuckles. "We're not your only legal firm." He pauses before pressing further. "But since we're discussing the subject, why did you buy the house?"

I shrug and answer, "It seemed like a good investment."

The truth is that Myka didn't want to sell, but in the end she went through with the sale because Shiloh decided to keep the babies. Her dream didn't come true—but one day, it will happen. Deep down, I'm almost certain she'll regret her decision to sell the house once she starts her family. And on that day, I'll happily sign the property back to her.

No one needs to know my plan—not even my cousin.

"It's okay to fall in love," Lang says, glancing at his husband. "Even I did."

"Listen, there's a lot I have to figure out. Teddy is still—"

"Teddy is doing fine. She's engaged and trying her best to live after everything that happened to her." He pauses, and I can sense his empathy for Teddy's struggles—or is it for me? "You can't use your siblings as an excuse to avoid life."

"So, what, you want me to date Myka?" I laugh, trying to shake off Lang's words. "I don't date."

He taps his chin, his expression thoughtful. "You're right," he admits, his eyes narrowing in on me. "She's probably not the right woman for you."

His words sting, and I can feel a twinge of hurt in my chest.

And to make things even worse, he adds, "You couldn't get a woman like her." The blunt statement hits me hard, and I can't help but feel a pang of inadequacy.

I cock a brow. "Is that a challenge?" My voice is laced with skepticism. What is he trying to accomplish? "Because I don't care to prove you wrong."

Lang shakes his head, his expression serious. "No," he says firmly, his lips pressed into a thin line. "It's a fact of life. She had a hard life, and you're definitely not what she needs."

I can feel a knot forming in my stomach as Lang's words sink in. A hard life?

I wonder if it has anything to do with the scars on her back. The thought sends a shiver down my spine. The time I asked her about it, she said it was an accident, but she didn't elaborate. I chose not to press the matter. But now, the question lingers in my mind.

Does it matter?

Do I care?

The answer is unclear, and I can feel a sense of unease settling in the pit of my stomach.

And maybe I do care. I care more than I want to admit.

Maybe Lang is right.

Maybe I can't keep using my siblings as an excuse to avoid living.

Maybe it's time to take a chance, to let go of my fears, and find happiness.

But where do I even start? How do I navigate this new territory? And what is happiness?

Then I look at Lang and his husband, and I see the love in their eyes.

And for the first time in a long time, I feel hopeful. Maybe it's okay to fall in love. Perhaps it's time to take a chance.

Isn't this why I've been going to a therapist? Not only to help my family, but myself.

Chapter Twenty-Six

Myka

"I WANT TO CALL MOM," Shiloh says on the other side of the line, her voice breaking.

"What's stopping you?" I ask quietly as I prepare my sandwich for dinner.

"She probably hates me," she cries out, and my heart aches for her.

I understand her apprehension all too well. My parents divorced when I was four. Mom left us and never came back to see us again. For years, I waited for her calls or visits, hoping she would be my birthday present, or my Christmas miracle. She never showed up.

There are rumors that she tried approaching us throughout the years, but Iskander and Manelik always stopped her. Although my brothers have good intentions, they need to stop making decisions about my life for me.

"Your fears are valid," I murmur reluctantly, "but maybe she regrets her actions and doesn't know how to get close to you. Why don't you give her a call?"

"What if she rejects me?" Her voice is small and fragile.

"No matter what happens," I assure her, "I'll be here for you."

A shuddering breath escapes her lips. "If my children ever make a mistake, I won't be like Mom or Dad."

I make my way to the dining table with my phone, plate, and glass in hand. "You're going to be a great mom," I promise softly as I take a seat. "It won't be easy, because parenthood is complicated, but you'll be great at it."

"Will you be here tomorrow?" she whispers shakily.

"Of course I will. I can't wait to meet the babies. Have you thought about any new names yet?" I take a bite of my sandwich and stare at my computer, debating if I should do some work today, or just wait until tomorrow and work during my flight to Portland.

Her voice cracks when she speaks again, "If they're boys, Bruin and Seahawk—those are my dad's favorite sport teams. If they're girls, Yaziel and Ambrose—they sound like fairies. If it's one of each… I'll pick from those four."

The names are still unconventional, but at least she

stopped including Grover, Loki, and Furious on her list this time around. Naming the boys after sports teams is something I've never heard before, but who knows what the new parents of today may come up with?

Since I don't want to mention that maybe she should rethink the names, I ask, "Is your hospital bag ready?"

"Yes," she answers. "And everything else is set for tomorrow. I was told that they won't send me to Seattle until the babies are two weeks old, just to make sure we're healthy."

"That's smart."

"How long will you stay here?"

I pause before answering. "How long would you like me to stay there?"

She pauses before answering hesitantly, "Until I head to Seattle?"

"I could do that. Why don't I call you tomorrow, before I board my plane?" I respond, opening my laptop and searching for an Airbnb where I can stay for that long. I need a place where I can work during the day and be myself. Hotels are too small, and I feel claustrophobic in them.

"Thank you again for being there for me. You'll be a good mom someday."

"Call if you need anything. If not, I'll see you soon," I say, hanging up the phone. As I'm browsing, a message pops on the right corner of the screen.

> Kingston: I'm finally heading to Seattle. Can we meet tomorrow night?

> Myka: :laughing: emoji.

Kingston: What did I say that's funny?

Myka: I'm leaving town tomorrow morning.

Kingston: You're toying with me.

Myka: No, I'm dead serious.

Kingston: I feel like ever since we changed our status from hookup to friends with benefits, you took away all the benefits. What's the deal with that?

Myka: Though I would love to say it's on purpose, it's not.

Kingston: When are you coming back?

Myka: A few weeks? I don't know. Shiloh wants me to stay in town with her until she's ready to travel to Seattle.

Kingston: Is she having the babies already?

Myka: Yes. That's why I'm leaving town tomorrow. Where are you?

Kingston: Myles and I are in Los Angeles, pretending we're visiting my branches. But in fact, we're waiting to see if Archer needs us.

Myka: Why would he need you? And isn't his name Finnegan now?

Kingston: :facepalm: emoji. I keep forgetting to call him by his new name. He's groveling to Piper, and his relationship is two or three degrees more complicated than before.

Myka: You're a good brother.

Myka: And as much as I want to continue chatting, I have to pack. See you around, St. James.

Kingston: See you soon. :wink: emoji.

Chapter Twenty-Seven

Myka

My morning doesn't go as planned. At eight in the morning, there's a driver at my door. He's been asked to take me to the hangar, where a private jet is waiting for me to fly me to Portland.

"Who hired you?" I ask suspiciously.

"I work for Kingston St. James. He's the one who requested me to be here with breakfast," he says, adding, "Which is downstairs in the car."

I could say no, that I already have plans. But for some reason, it's easier just to grab my bags and follow behind him.

When we get to the car, I text King, thanking him for this thoughtfulness, but he doesn't respond. During the short ride from Seattle to Portland, I take a nap instead of working.

When we land, I'm somehow nervous. I've been preparing myself to be Shiloh's support system, but I don't know if I can be the person she needs—a mother. The one I had was shitty, and I… well, I failed long ago. How can I be there for her?

"Stop those negative thoughts," I mumble under my breath.

"I can do this," I say as I step out of the private plane. My legs are slightly wobbly as I descend the stairs.

"Your luggage is already in the car," the flight attendant says when I reach the bottom of the staircase. I should ask what car, but I can't.

The uncertainty gnaws at me as I step off the plane. I know I'm supposed to be here to help, but I can't help feeling like a fraud. My palms sweat as I scan the area. That's when I spot a silver SUV. And of course, there's a guy leaning against it, crossed arms—Kingston St. James.

My heart pounds as I take in Kingston's appearance. He looks even better than I remembered but with an edge all of his own. My breath catches in my throat as he smirks at me, exuding confidence that only draws me closer.

But as much as I'm drawn to him, apprehension lurks beneath the surface. It has been so long since we've been together—what will this moment bring? When he kisses my cheek, my stomach flips with nerves, and I can't help but wonder.

What is he doing here?

"Umm… hello," I murmur, taken aback by his unexpected arrival. "Why are you here?"

He pauses before answering. "I thought you could use a friend while going through the adoption process."

"Oh…" I respond, surprised again. "She's keeping the children."

A look of confusion crosses his face. "Oh, I assumed she changed her mind and that's why you're here," he says, holding open the passenger door for me.

"I've been her support system for the past few weeks. It seemed logical to be here for her when she requested it," I explain, climbing inside the SUV.

He nods slowly, his brow furrowed. "So after she gives birth, what happens?"

"She's going to be in the hospital for five days after the C-section," I tell him, my voice low. I'm not sure if it's just sinking in that I'm not ready to be her support or if it's his presence that's making me feel uneasy. "And then we'll stay until she gets the green light to move to Seattle. She'll be living in a single parents shelter."

He furrows his brow and remains silent for a few moments, his eyes searching my face for any sign of doubt. Eventually, he asks in a low voice, "So you still don't get the babies?"

My heart sinks at his words, and I can feel tears prickling at the corners of my eyes. I shake my head, struggling to find the words to explain myself. "Shiloh is ready to take care of them."

He presses his lips together tightly and gives me a hesitant nod. I can almost feel Kingston's unease radiating from him, but I don't have the courage to ask what he's thinking. Does he think I'm weak for giving up so easily, or for still being around Shiloh, even though it may shatter my heart?

I inhale deeply and steel myself, then voice the question that has been building inside of me. "Are you mad at me?"

"No," he answers with a shake of his head. "Just baffled. She had support back in the shelter. Why did you feel like you had to take on the role of being a mother to her?"

"Maybe because I know what it's like to be without a mother as a teen," I reply, trying to make my tone sound lighthearted and omitting the rest of my reasons for helping her.

"So where are we going?" he asks.

I sigh, lacing my fingers together. "Listen, I appreciate that you're here, but—"

"Before you kick me out, let me just say something, okay?" He speaks faster than usual. His words are like a desperate plea.

"Uh-huh," I manage.

"I'm here to support you. I don't know you that well, but I know you try to avoid reaching out to your family."

"They're busy," I excuse my family.

"But I bet if you asked them to be here for you—"

"I don't need them," I interrupt him. "This isn't about me."

"Can I stay with you, please?" he asks.

I pause for a few moments before raising my head to meet his gaze, but he's focused on the road. If I'm honest with myself, the plea in his voice is enough for me to give in. I don't want to admit it, but being alone might be a bad idea. "Why do you want to do this?"

He throws his hands up in exasperation. "Fuck if I know, okay? All I know is that I want to be the one here for you when you need someone. Is that good enough of an explanation or not?"

My throat tightens and all I can manage is a whispery, "Thank you."

Chapter Twenty-Eight

Kingston

THE LAST TIME we came to the shelter, I barely took notice of my surroundings. My entire focus was on Myka and the news that she had decided to drastically change her life. I'm not judging her, but the news overwhelmed me. It was hard to know how to react and if she even wanted me around to support her.

Back then, she seemed like one of those people who would rather be alone. I'm starting to understand that she's just trying not to inconvenience anyone with her problems. She's independent, but she also makes a lot of assumptions about those who love her. I'm sure if she called her family, they would be here for her in a heartbeat.

It's sad that she's here just to care for Shiloh and not to become a mother. I believe that if there's someone who would be a wonderful mom, it would be her.

"Are you okay?" Myka asks when she notices my dazed expression.

Just now, I realize the shelter resembles an all-girls high school. I manage to nod before murmuring under my breath, "They're so young. I don't understand why they aren't home with their parents."

Myka stands beside me, her hands clasped before her, her expression one of sympathy mixed with sadness. "Not everyone is like your parents. Sure, they might have driven you crazy while growing up, but I bet they would've supported you if one of you had knocked up a girl—or Teddy ended up pregnant at that age."

Anger boils in my chest, and I clench my fists to keep from lashing out. No one here is responsible for the unfairness of their situation. "Who kicks out a minor from their home just because... pregnancies happen? Why not teach sex ed instead of pushing them away?" I growl angrily.

Myka shifts uncomfortably. Her eyes focused on the young women in the area. "I wouldn't... or abandon my child or... but then there are women who don't give you a second glance," she mutters under her breath.

"Your mom?" I ask, and she answers vaguely with a nod.

I don't know much about her mother.

I first met Iskander in third grade when his family moved

from Luna Harbor to Seattle. We became friends within days. I learned he lived with his dad, had three brothers and a little sister. Only once did he mention his mother—when he told us his parents were divorced. He never gave her a second thought.

If Myka feels the same about her as her brother, maybe she's not thinking about her mom and there's something else occupying her mind. I wish I had a stronger relationship with her so I could be of more help.

"Would you like to share with the class?" I prompt softly.

She shakes her head, staring at her shoes.

"It's me. You can trust me with anything," I insist.

She's lost in deep thought. I give her a moment, allowing her to gather her thoughts. Then I reach out and gently place my hand on her shoulder. "You don't have to share anything you're not comfortable with, but also know I'm here for you."

She nods, and we sit in silence for a few more moments. "I was nineteen," she whispers, clearing her throat to mask the emotions.

The weight in her unspoken words hangs heavy between us. After a long pause, she says, "Sorry, I don't think I'm ready…" Her voice trails, and her face suddenly changes when she sees Shiloh at the door.

Her smile is wide and her focus is on Shiloh. "Ready?"

"No. I don't think I'll ever be ready," Shiloh replies with a shake of her head before turning to me with an apologetic smile. "Hello, Mr. St. James. I didn't expect to see you here."

"Myka needed a ride to Portland, so I thought I'd tag along," I explain calmly.

Shiloh raises her brows in surprise. "Can we get a big breakfast first?" Shiloh's question is directed at me.

"Of course," I say at the same time Myka shakes her head. "You're scheduled to have surgery in three hours. You can't eat anything."

Shiloh's face droops like a sulky teen who just found out there's no dessert left in the fridge. "But it's my last meal before things get highly complicated. My life is about to change, and I need—"

"I don't want to sound like the rest of the staff, but you have to follow instructions," Myka says. "Which reminds me, did you get all the paperwork signed?"

"Yeaaah," she replies. Then, bites her bottom lip as she offers, hesitantly, "I spoke to Mom…"

"And?" Myka gently prods for more information.

Shiloh takes a deep, trembling breath before pressing on, her voice laced with a hint of wavering emotion. "We cried, and she said she might come to see me with Dad."

"I hope they do as promised," Myka says warmly.

A small grateful smile curls Shiloh's lips as she murmurs her gratitude toward Myk. "Thank you for being so cool with me."

WHEN WE ARRIVE at the hospital, Shiloh's parents are there. I want to be part of the conversation, but Myles texts me. We need to talk. I excuse myself and wait until I'm outside the hospital to call him.

"You took your sweet little time," he complains.

I scoff. "Why are you so dramatic?" I answer, then add slightly less annoyed, "How can I help you?"

"Mom knows," he mumbles.

"Is this the one where everyone knows—except me?" I ask confused.

He chuckles. "Why are you always in a bad mood?"

"Because you have to be too fucking cryptic. Can you just tell me what happened with Mom," I mumble.

"She knows Archer is alive," he mutters, releasing a groan. "She's freaking out, angry, and… did I tell you she's been calling everyone about this?"

"Not me," I say.

"Well, she was here earlier today, and I told her you were busy," he explains and then adds, "You're welcome."

"I'm not busy for her, if she's having a crisis."

"Can you come back home?" he asks.

I glance up toward the hospital where Myka is dealing with some kind of crisis of her own—alone. I can't leave her side, not even for a moment. Guilt and fear swirl inside me, a turbulence of conflicting emotions that leave me feeling trapped.

There shouldn't be a contest. Mom comes first. Myka is just the woman I spend some time with and… but my heart aches at the thought of leaving her, of walking away during an important moment of her life.

I take a breath, steadying myself before I answer, but Myles is the one who speaks, "King, I just want you to know what's happening. You don't have to come running home."

"But she needs me," I mutter.

"Correct me if I'm wrong, but I think Myka needs you more," he says in a low voice.

Yesterday, I told him about the adoption and everything that's been happening since… well probably since the Luna Harbor hookup. Neither one of us understands why she's going through this alone, but it doesn't matter. I'm here for her.

"Are the babies out yet?" he asks.

"You should say, have they been born, not out. I've yet to understand how you won so many awards for your documentaries when you don't even know how to speak properly."

"It's all the same," he says dismissively. "What about the babies?"

"We just arrived at the hospital. But…" I trail my words, take a deep breath, and then say, "Myk is here only to support her, not to adopt them. I'm pretty sure this is going to break her heart."

"You know how you can help her?" I wait for the punch line or some stupid comment. "Just knock her up."

I groan. "Seriously, Myles? What the fuck is wrong with you?"

"Me? You're the one who's being stupid. I'm giving you the best solution to solve the problem. The woman you love wants a baby—give her one."

"The who?" I ask, stumped by what he just said.

"Please tell me you're aware that you're in love with Myka Cantú." His voice comes out annoyed.

I freeze at his words, my heart pounding in my chest.

How does Myles know?

Is it that obvious that I am in love with her?

Chapter Twenty-Nine

Kingston

As I stand in place, my mind is filled with a jumble of conflicting emotions.

Love isn't a language I speak.

Falling for someone? It's unimaginable—especially not with someone like Myka.

She's a mystery, a puzzle unsolved. Everything I never knew I would desire.

Her presence alone is a sight to behold—a flame that sets my heart on fire.

I now realize that I ache with a deep sense of loss when she's not around. The fear of losing her grips my soul.

Myka is like a wildflower, a force of nature that cannot be tamed. She's unapologetically herself, and I find myself drawn to her in ways I can't explain. It's as if she sees through all of my defenses and straight into my soul, leaving me completely vulnerable.

This woman has single-handedly destroyed my armor, leaving my heart unprotected and at the mercy of her. And maybe I should hate her for what she's done, to lash out and push her away, but I couldn't fathom hurting her in any way.

All I can do is reconcile who I was and my former beliefs with… Fuck, I run a hand through my hair. I hate these emotions, my brother, and maybe myself.

I hate myself for not knowing what to do and for being afraid of what can happen.

The more I think about it, the more I realize that I can't imagine my life without her. She's become a part of me, and the thought of losing her is too much to bear. But the mere thought of confessing my love to her… it seems like the words are getting caught in my throat.

I'm torn between following my heart and trusting my head.

My head tells me to run, to remember what this is and what it isn't. This is not a romantic story. It's two people having fun and…

"Just give her the baby," comes through the phone, which I had forgotten was still in my hand. The possibility of having a baby brings relief yet terror at the same time. However, I'm tempted by Myles's suggestion. I would give the world to Myka, and more, if she so wished. If she asks for the stars, I will find a way to bring them to her.

But will she open up her world to me? What if I'm just like my father, and I end up hurting them both, the child and Myka?

The questions keep coming around in circles, and soon enough, I feel as though I can't breathe again.

Pushing my doubts aside, I focus on Myka. She's the most amazing woman I've ever met, and I want to give her everything she desires. But a baby… is that the right answer?

My throat catches as I whisper out, "I don't know if I can."

"You'll figure it out," Myles encourages me gently. "The first step is to acknowledge that you love her, and that's all that matters. Remember, you're not alone. I'm here for you."

Before I can ask him about Mom, I spot Myka leaving the hospital. "Hey, I'll call you later," I say without waiting for his response. I put the phone away and rush up to her.

Her eyes are flooded with tears, and her chin trembles. Did Shiloh's parents do something to her?

"Are you okay?" I ask anxiously, enfolding her in my arms.

She shakes her head no and sobs uncontrollably. I hold her tightly and wait until she is ready to tell me what happened. With every embrace and the delicate scent of flowers penetrating my senses, it validates what Myles said—I'm undeniably in love with this amazing woman and I can no longer deny it, nor do I want to.

She's such a beautiful and complicated person. Her heart is as deep as the ocean and as vast as the sky above us. Her emotions and feelings have no end, stretching out infinitely like the universe itself.

I've felt so drawn to the sheer magnitude of her being, which is a place of wonder, mystery, and depth.

Whenever I gaze into her eyes, I feel like I'm looking up at a starry night sky. It's like I'm looking into infinity, and I can't help but be mesmerized by the beauty and complexity of her. Every time we're together, I feel truly alive.

I know that there are so many layers to her, and I'm willing to explore each and every one of them. I want to delve deep into the depths of her soul and discover all the hidden corners and crevices that make her so unique.

But will she let me?

I fucking hope so, because without me noticing, I fell hard and irrevocably for her.

l love her fiercely.

If she allows it, I'll hold her close, kiss her softly every chance I have, and let her know that she's always safe with me.

I want to be her anchor in the storm, her safe haven in times of trouble, and her guiding light when she's lost in the darkness.

"What's going on, darling?" I whisper once she's calmed.

"They want… her parents convinced her to give up the babies," she sniffs. "But that's not what she wanted and also… they don't want to give them to me."

I pause, rubbing my hand soothingly against her back. "Why not?"

"I would be a single mother," she mumbles between sobs and adds, "Plus, it looks like

'I'm foreign,' and I probably don't have a penny to my name," she says, touching her beautiful olive skin.

"Those motherfuckers," I growl.

Before this, I hoped they were good people who just screwed up when they found out their kid was pregnant. Now, I see they're pieces of shit.

I'm so upset, I could punch a wall or scream until my throat is raw, but I understand that's not a reasonable solution to this problem. The adrenaline is pumping through my veins. How dare they speak like that to Myka, or treat their child as if she doesn't matter.

I take a deep breath and try to calm myself down, reminding myself that there are other ways to do things. "I'll show them what happens when they choose to disrespect their daughter, and mess with you."

"You could, but I'm not going to have you fight with them for me and try to prove that I'm worthy of them or their grandchildren—"

I press my lips tenderly against hers before pulling away. "So what do you want me to do?"

"Kick them out of the hospital? They're not good people. I can see them treating her poorly if she doesn't follow their rules," she says and adds, "But we can't do that. There's nothing that we can do. They threatened to call security on me if I didn't leave the premises."

"Shiloh did?" I confirm quietly, not wanting to make things harder for her by accusing her parents in front of her.

"No, she wanted me there. Her parents are the ones who ordered me to go away," she mumbles. "The nurses enforced the request because I'm not related, and I didn't want to complicate things with Shiloh. I just… we can't leave her with them."

"We can't," I agree emphatically before reaching for my phone.

Taking a deep breath, I immediately call Thea Decker. She should know what to do. After explaining the situation, she informs us that Shiloh has been emancipated for months now so it's ultimately her decision whether or not she signs the adoption papers. With that in mind, I place several more calls.

"What are you doing?" Myka inquires after I make a couple more calls, one of which is to my cousin Lang asking for legal help. Though he doesn't practice, his husband has a firm in Seattle and knows other lawyers in the Northwest.

I cast a sidelong glance at her and shrug noncommittally. "I'm not sure."

"You have the same crazy look Dad or Iskander do when they're about to finalize an acquisition," she says, and for the first time since we met this morning, she smiles. "What are you trying to accomplish here?"

"Who the fuck knows," I reply because if I'm being honest with myself, I don't know what I will accomplish with the team I'm assembling.

All I know is that there's a scared child about to give birth in the hospital. A kid who was abandoned by two inconsiderate bigots. I have to protect Shiloh from them. The rest… well, we'll figure out what will happen to her children once she's safe.

"You're adorable," Myka states softly, kissing my jaw.

A cynical chuckle crawls out of me. "Hardly."

"Well, can you at least tell me what you are doing?" She changes her question.

My voice intensifies with a newfound conviction. "I'm just here to show those people nobody messes with..." I pause, knowing I can't blurt out and declare my love for this woman.

Will I ever be brave enough to confess my feelings to her?

Or should I walk away and let her be happy with someone else?

Chapter Thirty

Kingston

M‌Y FAMILY'S response is overwhelming and unexpected. Within thirty minutes, a lawyer—Pierce Aldridge—arrives to represent Shiloh. His focus is to ensure that Shiloh's rights aren't violated by her parents or anyone in the hospital.

We have a private waiting room where Myka and I stay while they prep Shiloh. Thirty minutes after Pierce Aldridge arrived, Myles strides in with the whole family, including Finn who flew them from Seattle.

"Did you call everyone?" Myka asks nervously. She nibbles

on her bottom lip as the crowd continues to enter the private area.

I shake my head. "Only Lang, my assistant, and Myles," I answer.

As the crowd increases, she gives me a look that says, I'm overwhelmed, get me out of here.

Or maybe, I'm just making this up. Since I don't want to assume, I ask, "What's happening?"

She glances toward the door, then back at me. "Everyone is showing up. As you might remember, I haven't mentioned any of this to my family and—"

Before she can continue, someone calls out, interrupting her, "Mija." Her father enters along with a new wave of visitors behind him—her brothers.

Within seconds, he snatches her away from me, pulling her in and quickly wrapping her in his arms.

Myka glares at me, her eyes filled with icy contempt. I shrug nonchalantly and mumble, "It wasn't me," as I hurriedly retreat out of the area to avoid an argument with the Cantú men, who are very protective of her.

Just then, Finn strides toward me. He cocks his head and motions for me to follow him outside the waiting room. I can't help but wonder why he wants to speak to me. It would be nice if he's finally getting on board with our family again, but that sounds too good to be true.

"What's going on?" I ask, instead of just assuming.

"Piper is with Shiloh and the shelter's lawyer," he says, checking his phone. "We need to know what you or Myka need."

I arch an eyebrow and ask, "Though I appreciate your offer, somehow, I have the feeling that you're not here just to support me."

A derisive scoff escapes from his lips. "Pipe says that I have to do it because it's important to you." He pauses, pressing his lips and adding, "I'm still trying to get the handle of emotions and social cues."

I look at him suspiciously. "But that's not the whole thing, is it?"

He rolls his eyes. "I'm really here because someone had to fly everyone—including Piper and Derek." He mentions his partners. At least, I think that's what they are since he's dating both of them.

Maybe someday, he'll become part of us again, and we'll know what's happening in his daily life. For now, I should take whatever he offers us.

"Why is Piper even here?" Myles chimes in and when did he join the conversation?

Finn's lips curl into a half-smile. "She's representing the shelter and the interests of Shiloh alongside the lawyer. Derek and Seth are upstairs, ready to escort the girl's family out of the hospital if that's what she requests."

"Don't you work for a security company too?" I ask pointedly. "Shouldn't you be up there kicking them out?"

Finn lets out a chuckle. "Actually, I own it. And that's exactly what I suggested, but my man and my woman thought I'd be too lethal for this situation."

Lang joins us, nodding in agreement. "They would be right. Our man, Finn, doesn't know the difference between gently dismissing them and shooting them on their way out of here. He just shoots, no questions asked." Lang laughs at his stupid joke.

Finn's nostrils flare, but he doesn't say anything.

"Why are you here, Lang?" I ask, hoping he doesn't bother Finn. "I thought you already sent the lawyer to assist us."

"Nope," he says. "The lawyer I got was for Shiloh. Fitz is here to oversee the adoption if the girl decides to give them to Myk."

"Either way, we'll have security around the premises," Finn announces. "We'll be here to protect her until they're ready to leave the hospital. After that, the plan is to drive them to Seattle."

I furrow my brows, running a hand through my hair. "I thought they would stay here for a couple of weeks."

"It'll be better if they're out of the reach of Shiloh's parents," Lang explains. "We want to prevent any interactions between the girl and them."

We fall silent until I add one more thing. "Who involved Myka's family?" I stare at my cousin, since he's best friends with Manelik.

Lang shrugs. "You can't keep them in the dark with this kind of information. Mane knew most of it but was waiting for her to call. Plus, we were at Beacon's place when you called."

Finn scans the area and asks, "So where is Jayden?"

"Who?" I inquire, not recognizing the name.

"Jayden," he repeats. "I'm trying to understand what your role here is, if he's with her. Are the three of you together?"

Lang shakes his head. "The guy is not in the picture. Let it go."

"That doesn't make sense," Finn insists. "Just a few weeks ago, I read about him. I created an entire box for Pipe when Myka was kidnapped by the traffickers and she almost—"

"Shut up," Lang orders. "This is exactly what we mean when we say, get a clue, Finnegan Gil. Read the fucking room."

"Why are we not talking about him?" he asks, not letting this go. "He seemed like an important person to Myka… I mean, she almost died."

As Finn continues to push for answers, I can't help but to piece things together. She mentioned being part of The Organization when she was young, but she quit. I never pressured her to tell me the reason why she did it. I just let it go. She knew how to help Teddy, but it wasn't knowledge learned from somewhere, but from experience. It's clear that something traumatic happened to her.

This fills me with dread, and what am I supposed to do with this information?

My heart aches at the thought of her suffering, and I can't help but wish I could have been there to protect her and shield her from the pain and the trauma.

Then, I remember what Lang said, *You can't be the man for her.*

He doesn't believe I can become who she needs because my father couldn't handle what happened to my mother and he destroyed our entire family. I should walk away. I won't do any damage to the woman I love. Without a word, I walk away.

Chapter Thirty-One

Myka

PA'S GRIP tightens on my hand before releasing it. My brothers exchange meaningful glances—I can feel their silent judgment weighing down on me. "I don't understand why you didn't trust us," Pa complains, his voice full of disappointment.

"There was nothing to say," I argue and explain everything that had transpired. From the moment I received the first call until the moment they'd arrived.

Mane pulls me into a hug, asking in a low voice, "Why do

you attract so much drama?" The idiot chuckles as if his comment will lighten up the mood.

"It's a gift," I sigh, trying not to grumble.

"In my opinion—" Iskander says, but it's interrupted by an eerie silence. I lift my gaze and find Piper and Grace approaching me.

Their faces are grim. Piper speaks first, "Shiloh wants you and King to be with her during childbirth."

My eyes snap to hers. "Her parents?" I hear the fear in my own voice. I don't want to be in the same room as them. It took a lot of self-control to make sure I didn't snap at them.

Grace answers solemnly, "They've been escorted off the premises."

My gaze darts around the room, searching for Kingston, but he isn't here. Earlier he disappeared with Finn and I haven't seen him since. As if Piper had read my mind, she explains that Finn is getting him. "Why don't I take you to the OR? You can put on some scrubs."

Pa reaches for my hand once more and squeezes it tenderly. "We'll be here waiting for you."

"What happened with Shiloh?" I ask, as I follow Grace and Piper to the elevator.

Grace shares a knowing look with Piper before responding with a low and gentle tone, "All you need to know is that the parents are out of the picture. There are certain legal issues we'll handle." She pauses and adds, "You don't have to worry about any of it."

"Is Shiloh okay?" Concern fills my voice.

"She's better now," Grace whispers. "My sister-in-law is

with her and will assist during the procedure. Blaire is a physician's assistant."

Piper quickly checks her phone, then looks up at us. "D needs me. I'll meet you upstairs."

Confusion crosses my face. "Who is D?"

Grace smiles. "Derek Farrow. You'll meet him later—he's with Finn and Pipe. Can you try to smile or at least tell me what's happening."

"So, I'm guessing things didn't go according to plan," I say as we step onto the elevator, my nerves on edge. There are too many people in here, and I'm so conflicted. This would be a good time to call my therapist. But I'm not the one who needs help. I sigh, mumbling, "Shiloh was hoping for reconciliation with her parents."

As we ascend, I desperately try to push away the worry and anxiety coiling around me. This isn't about me. There's a kid who needs me, and I have to be present for her. I can't fall apart because this situation feels too close and personal.

"Piper thinks they only came here to restore their reputation and not take her and the children with them," Grace remarks, breaking through my thoughts. "But that's just a guess. You can discuss this with her once the babies are born, and she's in a better place."

I nod, wanting nothing more than for Shiloh to be okay—I'd never do anything to make her uncomfortable. Grace takes my hand in hers, giving it a reassuring squeeze. "You alright?"

"Of course, why wouldn't I be?"

She gives me "the look," one that says all too clearly that this must remind me of my mother, and... I swallow hard, refusing to remember the second part. But Grace knows all about it. She and I used to be best friends. We had a strong bond. But things were never the same after what happened to me. I stayed away from everyone and pushed them as far away as I could.

"Zoey would have been fifteen now," she murmurs, apparently thinking about *her* too. "It doesn't take a genius to figure out why you've been looking after this child—she reminds you of your daughter."

"That has nothing to do with it," I retort, but my voice is defensive and bitter.

"You can deny it, but we know that's why," she insists. "Aunt Thea brought us up to date on everything that's been happening since she contacted you. I wanted to yell at her for dragging you into this drama, but then, I realized you're the best person to look after this girl."

"This has nothing to do with Zoey. She died, and if she had lived, he would've taken her away from me," I mumble underneath my breath. "I wasn't fit to be a mother—I got her killed."

Grace stops the elevator abruptly and looks me dead in the eye with an intensity that nearly makes me break down right then and there. "It wasn't like that," she rebuts, her voice full of emotion. "Please tell me you don't believe it. If you had known you were pregnant, you wouldn't have been there."

My own emotions come bubbling up as I reflect on my terrible past. "But later, while I was captive..." I don't know how to finish this sentence. I tried my best to fight them, but that's what got me into their dungeon. I was no longer someone they wanted to sell to the highest bidder but someone they used and abused. They...

I have to take a long breath and remind myself that I'm not there. I got out alive—but then, my little girl died. She didn't survive everything that was done to my body.

Her voice trembles as she speaks. "I wish it had been me... or that I had reached you in time. As much as I try to remember that I didn't fail, I feel as if I failed you both."

"But you didn't," I whisper.

"You're right. It wasn't anyone's fault," she states firmly as tears stream down her cheeks and trickle onto mine. We both cry until our eyes are empty.

The elevator resumes its way up. We step out when we arrive at our destination. And as I march down the hallway, my heart sinks as I'm overcome by a wave of grief that crashes into me like an avalanche. All I can focus on is the past and the pain of losing my daughter, relentlessly beating against me with every step.

Zoey would be fifteen now. I wonder what she would look like, what kind of person she would have become. Would she be strong and independent like me, or would she take after her father? I'll never know.

Her memory floods in, and I shudder at the thought of what she could have been. These questions will forever remain unanswered.

The guilt sits firmly on my shoulders like a heavy stone, crushing me under its weight. If only I had known about the pregnancy, if only I had been more careful... maybe then, my sweet angel could still be alive today.

It's a pain that never truly goes away. Every day, I'm reminded of her absence, and it feels like a part of me is missing. Taking care of Shiloh isn't an act of redemption, but a way to give some of the motherly love that's wasted inside of me.

I try to push the thoughts aside, but they keep creeping back in. I'm not strong enough to handle it all. But then I remember the promise I made to myself, the promise to be there for Shiloh, to protect her the way I would if Zoey was in her shoes.

It's not about me. It's about her, and her children. I'll do whatever it takes to keep her safe—even if it means reliving the pain of losing my daughter over and over again.

Chapter Thirty-Two

Kingston

"Where the hell do you think you're going?" Finn demands, voice loud and echoing through the parking lot.

I pause mid-stride, turning to face him. "Home," I answer, my tone hollow. "She doesn't need a fuckup like me."

His lips quirk into a grin that reminds me of the old Archer. "Have you always been this melodramatic?"

I fix my eyes on him with a piercing stare, and in turn, Finn reciprocates my glare. "Are we engaging in some kind of competition here?" he asks amused.

I feel my annoyance building up and my nostrils flare up. "You were supposed to back off," I say, trying to keep my cool.

He laughs and shakes his head, his gray eyes glinting mischievously in the late morning sun. This reminds me of the old Archer. He would be playful and almost laughing at everything, even during serious matters. It was his way to make others feel at ease.

"So, according to you, I back down and then apologize for…" He shrugs and shakes his head. "I don't have time for your nonsense. I need to understand why you left the hospital. One moment you're making calls to ensure Myka and the girl who she's helping get justice, and the next, you're leaving like a scaredy-cat."

"You wouldn't understand," I respond, taking a step back and moving away from him.

He uncrosses his arms and gives me a skeptical look. "Having amnesia doesn't mean that my IQ dropped. I'm pretty sure I can keep up with any 'complicated issues' you might have," he scoffs.

My cheeks burn with shame, and I look down at my shoes instead of meeting his gaze. "Our father—"

"Your father," he corrects me sternly and deliberately stares at me until it's clear that I won't be saying anything else on the subject. It's so hard to get used to this new version of my brother. This Finnegan person has his face and sometimes brings up his old quirks, but he's not Archer. He is a different man.

"Why do you even care about this situation?" I snap at him.

"I was told this is important to you," he responds, shrugging. "If there's something I've learned in the past few weeks, it's that *you* would do anything for your family—including young me. I'm learning to care about you, and this is a good exercise."

Finn stares at me thoughtfully for a few seconds before cracking a smirk and murmuring, "In a way, you're doing me a favor."

My jaw clenches in irritation. "You're frustrating."

"We know why I behave out of the norm." He touches his head. "I lived with wolves and had to do bad stuff to survive. Now that I'm back in this world, I'm learning to follow social norms. But you... can you give me a play-by-play of these daddy issues?"

I tell him about our parents' screwed-up marriage. How we all caught them cheating on each other, and they didn't divorce until Teddy turned eighteen. "Only a few months ago we learned this was because Mom..." I close my eyes and tell him what we learned.

"Sorry about what happened to your mom," he mumbles.

I want to tell him that she's his mother too and he should try to accept her. Instead, I say, "She's working through it."

Finn nods slowly but says, "So we don't know who Jayden is, but we assume something bad happened to Myka. Therefore, you think you'll behave like Donovan?"

"You're catching on."

"Yes, I've always been the smartest of the St. Jameses." He taps his temple. "Even with my social problems and the fact that I can't remember being a part of the family, I can understand that what you're saying is stupid."

"No," I start to say, but then Piper suddenly appears in front of us.

"What happened?" I ask, fearful of what could have caused her to run so fast.

"You. I got a '9-1-1 idiot on the loose,'" she says breathlessly, then holds up her phone to show me a text.

"Myka doesn't need me here," I mutter inwardly.

"Somehow, I think you're wrong. Shiloh wants you and Myka to be there when the babies are born." She gives me a challenging look and asks, "Why did you decide you're not useful?"

I hang my head in shame. "I'm not sure what happened to her, but I don't think I'm strong enough to be around her," I mumble.

"He thinks he's like Donovan," Finn complements my response, rolling his eyes.

"Oh," she says, shaking her head. "Your father isn't a bad man. He's... not the problem right now. Focus on Myka."

Finn's curiosity piques as he questions, "So who is Jayden, and why isn't he here?"

"He dated Myka when they were in high school." Piper draws in a ragged breath, her eyes dulling with the painful memory. "It was a horrible breakup. I can't go into details, but... Myka was kidnapped. It was worse than what happened to Teddy." She drops her gaze to the floor, her voice barely audible as she whispers, "It was so much worse."

I'm trying to keep up with her answer, and as more pieces fall into place, it confirms my fear. She lived through the same things Teddy did and the man who was supposed to be with her, being her rock and support, just left her.

Piper continues haltingly, "There was a baby daughter, too—Zoey." Her tears fall freely as she states softly, "She passed away a few days after being born prematurely, and Jayden couldn't handle it. He blamed Myka for what happened to Zoey." Her voice chokes on the last words, and she swallows hard before adding, "She would be fifteen now.

"If you have to leave, do it now. We don't need someone weak to drag her to hell, the way Jayden did," Piper states almost coldly.

Anger rushes through me at her urging, and I glare at her fiercely. "You're a pain in the ass," I snarl before turning away from her and making my way back to the hospital.

I hear the sound of skin slapping, and when I turn around, I catch Piper and Finn high-fiving each other, the same way they used to do when they were younger. And I smile, knowing that after the heartbreak of losing my brother, Piper was still able to fall in love with the man he became. Not only that, but they found love with Derek Farrow too. It's hard to understand their dynamic, but the times I've seen them together, I sense their happiness and their love—and that's all that matters to me.

When I'm by the hospital entrance, Iskander stands, glaring at me. "Good, you got your act together. I'm not sure what's going on between you and my sister, but if you leave her without an explanation, I swear, I'll find you and kill you with my bare hands."

"Is the threat necessary?"

"Probably not, but... seriously, you've been sleeping with my sister." He pauses and glares at me. "What kind of man screws around with his best friend's little sister?"

"Though we're friends, again, I don't think you can say we're best friends, yet. Also, I'm not screwing around with her. I'm—" I clamp my mouth and take a breath. "This is a conversation I need to have with her, not you. Just know this is fucking serious for me. She's important."

"Good to hear. Still, you hurt her, and you'll have a problem with the Cantú brothers."

I wave at him and head toward the elevator. He can wait for another day. Myk needs me, and she's all that matters.

Chapter Thirty-Three

Kingston

"Your eyes are blotchy," I say softly, adjusting my scrubs as we prepare to enter the operating room. "What happened?"

Myka shrugs, avoiding my gaze.

I take a step toward her, reaching out. "Myk?"

"Shiloh is waiting for us," she replies quietly, her voice barely audible over the hum of hospital machinery.

I grasp her hand and squeeze it gently before placing a soft kiss on her cheek. She briefly closes her eyes at my touch. "I'm here, okay. Always."

She looks away for a moment before murmuring, "They told you, didn't they?"

"Does it matter?" I ask, pulling her into an embrace.

"This isn't how I do things." The sadness in Myka's voice carries an unbearable weight. "If Shiloh hadn't asked for you, I would beg you to leave."

"You could, and I'd do it. Because all I want is for you to be happy, but…" I pause, taking a deep breath. "We're also good at breaking Myka's rules, aren't we? All in the name of making you happy."

She pulls away a little, taking a deep breath. Her gaze is direct and unyielding when she speaks again. "You should leave."

"I could," I murmur agreeably as I brush my lips along her earlobe, my words barely audible. "But the last thing I want to do is leave the woman I love when she needs me."

And this is probably the worst time to tell her how I feel and what she means to me, but is there ever a good time for that in a situation like this?

A sigh escapes her throat as she turns slightly away from me. "King…"

I feel the shift in the air. I know she's about to lash out or do something to push me away. I'm aware because we're not so different when it comes to feelings. We avoid emotions. Neither one of us wants to be a part of a couple, both afraid to hurt or be hurt.

The thought of her leaving fills me with a sense of desperation and fear I never thought I would ever experience. I want to hold her tight, to tell her that everything will be alright and that I will always be here for her. But this isn't the time. I have to wait and hope she doesn't retreat into herself and break us both into a million pieces.

I lean back, trying to lighten the mood with a little humor, as my siblings do from time to time. Without breaking eye contact, I let out a sigh and give her an amused smirk. "Yeah… I know. You told me not to fall," I shrug and add mockingly, my tone conveying the message: I'm an idiot, I know. "I tried my best, but as you know, I don't follow instructions very well. And I failed miserably at this *not falling* thing. You set me up for failure—you demolished all my barriers, stole my heart, and made me need you."

Myka's lips twitch into a small smile as she adjusts her mask, her expression unreadable. Something electric passes between us. "That's a mistake," she says gravely. "You should rethink this because I'm incapable of love—as your cousin puts it, I'm a coldhearted bitch."

She's wrong. Myka can try her damn best to hide who she is behind her icy façade, but only someone who loves deeply could be so scared of loving again. She'll see it when she's ready.

"It's fine," I say casually in an effort to keep things light. "I can love enough for the both of us in this relationship. At least until you're ready." To reassure her that there's no pressure from my end, I offer her one last wink before putting on my scrubs and facial mask.

Myka merely looks at me skeptically, an eyebrow raised in

challenge. "You think you're so cocky now," she scoffs, "but nothing is going to happen between you and me."

I reply confidently, "No. It will, I'm that sure about us." Then, gesturing toward the room where our friend Shiloh awaits us, I add lightly, "Let's help Shiloh first, then we can discuss new ways to give you some children later today."

I DESERVE A PRIZE FOR THIS. There's a reason why I can never even consider becoming a doctor: I'm not a fan of hospitals, blood, or the scent of antiseptics. They fill me with dread, not to mention the intense pressure and responsibility that comes with the role. It takes a miracle and the reminder that someone is counting on me to keep my breakfast down and my legs from shaking.

The doctor asks Myka if she'd like to cut one of the umbilical cords while he requests me to cut the second one. It feels like cutting into a sponge, but before I can protest or think it's gross, all I see is the little boy staring at me, tears streaming down his red face as he cries out loud.

As I stretch out my hand to touch his tiny palm, I assure him gently, "It's alright. Everything will be okay." He sobs a couple more times before finally calming down.

Myka nudges her head toward the corner where the nurses had taken the babies for cleanup. She murmurs, "Keep an eye on them." Although I'm not sure what for, I obey without question.

When the nurses put small bracelets on their feet, panic claws up my throat because I'm afraid these will hurt them somehow. But instead of taking them off as soon as I say so, one of them puts two on my left wrist too. What are they doing?

"Is this necessary?" I ask.

"Of course it is," the nurse answers. "This tells the medical personnel that you're their parent."

Another nurse huffs and rolls her eyes. "Newbies," she says with an exasperated voice. Then, she adds, "The babies are going to the room."

The doctor says, "I'm almost done. Then, we'll take the mom to the recovery room."

"I'll follow them." Myka gives Shiloh's hand a gentle squeeze and says, "You did great."

Shiloh looks up at me with shadowed eyes before calling out softly, "Mr. St. James…"

I spin around with a smile that doesn't quite reach my eyes. "Kingston," I correct her gently. "The name is Kingston."

She pauses for a beat before continuing quietly, "When are you telling her?"

I cock an eyebrow in confusion. "What exactly are we talking about?"

"That you're in love with Myka," she says. "And I'm wondering if she gets the babies, will you…?" She trails off, waiting for an answer.

My heart sinks into my stomach and my jaw clenches. With great effort, I steady my voice and say firmly, "Don't toy with her. It will break her heart if you make promises you don't intend to keep."

Shiloh pauses for a moment before responding. "I think she'd do a better job than me," she replies quietly.

I arch an eyebrow in surprise. "Why the sudden change of mind?"

She takes a deep breath before continuing dejectedly, "I'm not even seventeen yet. I could try my best but will I be a good mom?"

"I think you're capable of it. And you have a good support system," I remind her.

"Probably, but I think they will be better off with someone like Myka. You were right. She's full of love."

"Listen," I suggest, "why don't you take some time to think it over for a couple of days, and then we'll help you with whatever you decide."

Her gaze flicks toward mine, and she whispers with uncertainty, "But if she keeps them, will you care for them?"

My eyes drop involuntarily to the bracelets that had been entrusted to me without any questions asked. Would I really be capable of looking after these children? If they're willing to let me—yes, I believe I can give it my best shot. Looking back up at her, I admit solemnly, "I can only promise to love them as if they were mine. I can't guarantee I won't make mistakes, but if you and Myk allow it, I'll try my best to be a good father."

Her lips curl up slightly in acknowledgment before she looks across the room at the physician's assistant and declares firmly, "I can go now."

As they roll the bed out of the room, I feel a lump form in

my throat. This moment feels so final, so irreversible. In less than a day, my life seems to be shifting, and I have to face everything that I've avoided during my adult life. Love, having a family of my own... Will I be able to convince Myka to let me into her heart?

Am I enough for her?

Chapter Thirty-Four

Myka

Boys.

Two healthy, beautiful boys.

"You are perfect," I say as I admire them. The nurse just brought them to the room. Shiloh is recovering from surgery and should be here in a few hours.

The first baby is sleeping soundly, his little chest rising and falling with each breath. He has a head full of dark hair, and his cheeks are round and chubby.

The second baby is awake but I doubt he's aware of everything that's happening here. He has a little tuft of brown hair on the top of his head, and his hands are waving around as if he's trying to grab on to something. Should I wrap him? Why didn't they bundle him the way they did with his brother? As I admire their beauty, I swallow hard, trying to ease the lump that has formed in my throat.

I reach out and gently touch the soft skin of the baby's hands. It's warm and delicate, and I feel a surge of love and protectiveness wash over me. Carefully, I wrap the baby with the blanket. "You should go to sleep like your brother."

He makes a coo sound that melts my heart. "I want one," I mumble.

All of a sudden, I become aware of the sound of someone clearing their throat behind me, and when I turn around, I see that it is Kingston. "The janitor's closet is just around the corner. We could try to make one." His voice is low and suggestive.

Those words just remind me of our conversation before the babies were born. He said he loves me… and he knows about my past. I'm dizzy with confusion, and rage. Who told him about my past? And how much does he know?

Is he just going to be with me because he pities me? I don't want to pursue a relationship with anyone. But when I glance at him, I see the man who's been by my side for months.

But I can't be in a relationship, I repeat inside my head.

Sure, he's sweet, kind, and honest. He's intelligent and ambitious, and… even when I want to deny it, there's always been a connection between us—not only physical but emotional.

My heart feels like it's about to burst out of my chest. I'm consumed with conflicting emotions, torn between the fear of being vulnerable and the overwhelming desire to give in to his love. The thought of losing him terrifies me, but the idea of being hurt again is even worse.

My chest heaves as I grapple with the inner turmoil boiling within me. I can't help but wonder if he's the one who will finally break into the shield of ice that's wrapped around my heart. The possibility of a future with him fills me with both excitement and apprehension.

There's no denying the magnetic pull between us, yet I'm determined to conceal the emotions he seeks to evoke from within me.

I shake my head. "I wouldn't trust myself with a kid of my own," I state aloud, hoping the harsh truth will frighten him away.

"Do you want to talk about it?" his deep voice inquires gently.

My lips part, and my whisper carries out of them like a breeze. "We named her Zoey. She was born premature—twenty-three weeks—but sadly, she only survived five days. I wasn't even there in her final moments."

As he nears me, his strong arms pull me into his chest in a tight embrace, providing me with warmth and safety. His gentle touch soothes my spirit as I melt against him. "I'm sorry for your loss," he murmurs into my hair.

The guilt grasps me by the throat. Like every day, it tightens its grip with each passing moment I allow myself to remember her. It's like a vise, squeezing the air out of my lungs, asphyxiating me with remorse and self-blame. I can't escape the nagging feeling that I am responsible for what happened and could have done something to prevent it. No amount of counselors, self-help books, or… nothing erases the survivor's guilt.

I lived, and she died.

I put her in danger, and she couldn't become a person. Until now, I still wonder who she would have become if she had survived. But I also condemn myself because it's my fault that we'll never find out.

"What happened to Zoey's dad?" he wonders quietly.

Swallowing thickly, I admit dejectedly, "He blamed me for it all… If only I had stayed home in Seattle instead of going out partying with my brother…" My words hang heavily in the air as shame and regret course through my veins.

"He didn't know I worked for The Organization. That I had chosen to go to school in New York so I could be close to my team," I explain to him, because there was never partying around there. We just trained, studied, and went to school. "I never told him I was an agent—I doubt he even knows the company exists."

A wave of fury washes over King's face as his expression hardens. "Wait, so after you were attacked, lost your baby, and were trying to recover… the jerk blamed you?" His voice is low and deep and full of fury.

I rest my head against his chest and let the tears fall freely onto his shirt. The heat pouring off of him warms me.

"To be honest, I'm still learning about emotions and love," he murmurs, stroking my hair gently. "But just know I love you with all my heart. I'm here in any capacity you'll allow, but if I can help it, I'll never leave your side."

"I'm not a good person. You should stay away."

King kisses my temple tenderly, embracing me even closer. "I'm not going anywhere," he insists. "You can push me away, but I'll still be right beside you—unless you explicitly tell me to leave because you can't ever love me."

He wraps his arms around me firmly, squeezing my body close to his, and whispers in my ear, "You'll never have to face anything alone again. I'll always be here for you. Because I love you and I don't want to live without you."

I slowly lift my gaze up to meet his eyes, a spark of surprise glinting amidst the sorrow. Maybe he's not the only one who failed at following instructions.

But to love again… My heart doesn't feel safe. It quivers in fear like it's been trapped behind the bars of a prison cell with thousands of razor-sharp knives pressing against its broken pieces that once held so much warmth and light. One false move and it could shatter into tiny fragments that can never be taken back.

I take a deep breath to calm my racing pulse and try to loosen the tightness constricting my chest as if I'm suffocating beneath the pressure. The thought of loving again makes me feel vulnerable, exposed to all the ways King might be able to hurt me.

"I didn't confess my love for you to upset you," he murmurs, his voice warm and familiar and comforting like a blanket on a cold winter night. "The last thing I want to do is to hurt you, Myk."

His voice, his embrace… Everything about this man reminds me of the past few months. He's been by my side, leaning on me and sometimes letting me lean on him. A flicker of light in the darkness. Maybe, just maybe, my heart can be safe again. Maybe those knives can be dulled—blunted until they can no longer harm me.

I finally find comfort in allowing myself to love again.

And with that thought, a torrent of tears spills from my eyes. Ugly, uncontrollable sobs wrack my body, releasing all the pent-up emotions that have detracted from my soul for far too long. But even as I cry, I feel a sense of relief—a release knowing that maybe it's okay to allow him in, to stop denying my feelings for Kingston St. James.

Chapter Thirty-Five

Myka

"Do we have names for the twins yet?" Pa asks as he's helping change the diaper of baby one.

"It's Thing-One and Thing-Two," Myles replies as he feeds... Well, Thing-Two.

"She hasn't made any decisions yet," I reply, my voice low. "Her mother wasn't thrilled about the original names, and now she wants to find something perfect."

I cringe inwardly at the thought of Lang reminding us that they must be registered before leaving the hospital. Thankfully, he isn't here right now, no doubt lecturing Shiloh on all the paperwork she has yet to complete. The response of family and friends is overwhelming—Ainsley Bradley even arrived last night and assigned everyone duties.

Manelik's friend owns the Merkel Hotel a few blocks from here and blocked an entire floor just for our use. He closed a restaurant specifically for all the people who were staying to help take care of Shiloh and her newborns.

I'm overwhelmed with love and also thankful that for the past two days, we've had so many people around that King and I haven't found time to discuss the future of us. Maybe I can wait until things settle down before I can make sense of all these tumultuous emotions again: Do I love him? Yes, but can we work it out?

"Babe." King's voice interrupts my musings. When I turn around, he's peeking through the doorframe with a look that simultaneously warms my heart and makes me nervous. "Can you come over for a second? Shiloh wants to speak with us."

"Is she okay?" I ask, genuine concern reflected in my voice.

He nods, taking my hand and leading me to the room next door. Shiloh is in the bed, playing with the Nintendo Switch King brought her yesterday. He's spoiling her a lot—everyone is. And I'm glad that she's being loved, more so after her parents were so nasty with her.

"How do you feel?" I ask softly, unable to stop myself from tucking a strand of hair behind her ear. "You look far better than yesterday—have you been eating properly?"

"Oh, you're such a mother hen." Shiloh releases a throaty chuckle.

"Sorry, it's just…"

"It's alright. I'm grateful for everything you and King have done for me—my parents never pampered me like this."

While we attempt to make her comfortable here, I remind her of her responsibilities. I gesture toward the books King had bought just yesterday. "You need to decide on names for them soon."

"Why don't you do it?" she offers hopefully.

I shake my head firmly and say, "Though it would be an honor, I think you should be the one choosing them."

King clears his throat, giving a stern look at Shiloh.

She presses her lips together, then takes a deep breath before saying: "What I mean to say is that I'd love it if you two adopt them."

My eyebrows shoot up in surprise as I take in her words. "You want me to co-parent with him?"

"Usually partners co-parent. But what do I know? I'm just a child." Her eyes twinkle with amusement as she sasses me.

I purse my lips, trying not to laugh too but failing miserably as I reply, "He's not my—"

Shiloh interrupts me before I can finish my sentence, "Well, you two should solve that part too. I mean he loves you and you love him. What other good reason is there for being together? Do you have any reasons not to?"

King laughs lightly at her comment, then adds, "She has a valid point."

"You don't like children. What happened to being allergic and not in your—"

King turns toward me with a warm smile on his handsome

face. "That was young Kingston, full of fear and scared of falling in love. I'm a better version of that man." He grins at me. "I'm not planning on proposing to you because we have a lot to discuss, but I hope you'll give us a chance."

"This is too much to take in," I mumble, holding my stomach.

Shiloh looks at me expectantly. "I hope you don't regret wanting them."

"Why do you want to give them up?"

She gives me a sad smile. "I'm not mature enough to do it and even when I want to love them. I see them and... I don't want to resent them—or for them to resent me. They deserve good parents who're ready for them."

I glance at Kingston, who mouths, "We're ready." Then clears his throat and says, "The three of them need us."

He's right. Shiloh is asking for support, and I get to love three people and welcome them as part of our family. I don't know how this will work, but I think we can do it.

"Can we do it?" I ask.

King walks close to me, takes me into his arms, and kisses me. The world around us fades away, and all that's left is the thudding of our hearts, beating in perfect sync. With every breath, I feel his love pouring into me, a steady stream of devotion that leaves me breathless. I realize then that this kiss is a promise. A promise that no matter what happens, we'll face it together.

That this is the beginning of us. As we break apart, my eyes lock onto him, and I can see the love and passion reflected back at me. In that instant, I know that we're ready.

"Are you sure about this?" I ask again as we enter the room to see them again, but for the first time as ours.

"Only if you are," King mumbles, taking Thing-One away from Dad and placing him on top of his chest. "We're ready, aren't we, little one?"

"What happened?" Pa asks.

I suck my bottom lip before saying, "Shiloh wants us to adopt them."

"Welcome to the family," Myles mumbles at Thing-Two. "I will be your favorite uncle. Just because Fletch is a football player, it doesn't mean he's more fun than me. Do you understand?"

"You know he has other uncles," Pa says, and because all Cantús are competitive, even he will make them work for it.

"Of course, you say that because you're going to be the favorite grandfather," Myles argues, standing up and handing me the baby. "I'll buy you lunch to discuss this arrangement, Mr. Cantú."

Once they close the door behind them, I take a good look at us—what is our new little family. And it finally hits me, the enormity of this moment, of the offer, and I start to cry—again.

"What's wrong, Myk?"

"I don't know," I sob. "This is too good to be true, and I know I deserve it, but…"

"We'll work through this together, okay. We're yours to love."

"Where are we going to live?"

He gives me the typical St. James grin. "Leave it to me, but do you have any pictures of your old house... and maybe a nursery?"

"Like images of nurseries?" I ask, wiping the tears with the back of my hand.

"Yes, something like that." He kisses the forehead of the baby he's holding and sets him in his crib. "We also need names for you two. I don't know how Aunt Teddy was able to bring so many outfits for Thing-One and Thing-Two, but we won't let her do this forever, will we?"

I laugh and I set the baby in the plastic crib and send him my Pinterest. Then, pull out the list of names I picked back when I hoped Shiloh would choose me. We pick Ezra and Lance.

Ezra and Lance Cantú-St. James.

This feels surreal, but instead of being doubtful, I feel like we can make this work.

Chapter Thirty-Six

Myka

TWO WEEKS after the babies enter the world, we're allowed to return home. I assumed it was Seattle until we land in San Diego. I don't know what to expect, but then, I catch sight of my old house.

"Umm, you do remember I sold this place?" I whisper, peering up at King.

He grins at me, creases fanning out around his eyes. "Of course I do. You kept increasing the price so I wouldn't buy it."

"You... it was you?" My voice trembles with awe as understanding dawns on me.

He nods, a sly smile curving his lips. "Who else would give it back to you if you had any seller's remorse?"

I don't know how to express what I'm feeling, so I just say, "I love you, St. James."

Shock radiates from him and he gapes at me. "You do?"

My heart thrums in my chest with an intensity that rivals thunder. "It's impossible not to when you've been nothing but amazing from the beginning."

"I wouldn't call myself that, but..." He shrugs a shoulder. "There's something about you... I think my heart knew it was safe with you."

A knock on the car window startles us from our private moment and Finn peers in, wearing a cap and sunglasses. Is he hiding from something? "I hate to interrupt, but some of us are waiting for you." He doesn't say more and opens the passenger door to pull out one of the car seats.

"I thought you were on a mission," I say, getting down from the car.

Piper trails behind him, hefting the other car seat. "We said project not mission. Teddy recruited us."

Not bothering to question their response further, I grab one of the diaper bags and follow them inside.

When we enter the house, my breath catches in my throat. The place looks exactly like my old house did—except with a few modern details thrown in here and there. The furniture is brand new and Teddy practically dances with joy as she shows me all the work they'd done on the house based off my

Pinterest boards. They had even torn down a wall between two bedrooms to create a big nursery for the babies.

"This is perfect," I breathe, taking in every detail of the blue and gray décor.

"You created it," Teddy declares, picking up a remote control. Suddenly, the shutters close and she whispers, "Stars on."

As if right on cue, twinkling lights burst across the walls.

"Seth and Finn created that," Teddy says with pride. "It's like the old days: You put them together, and they're ready to make some magic."

"Where are my babies?" I inquire, remembering Piper had mentioned something about them earlier.

"Oh, there are a few guests in the backyard," Teddy stammers nervously. "I asked them to wait, but some of them were dying to welcome Ezra and Lance to the family."

Taking my leave from her, I descend downstairs and bump into Grace who holds Lance in her arms. "Congratulations," she gushes.

"Thank you…" I respond softly.

"I didn't do anything," Grace admits sheepishly, "but I hope this gives us a chance to mend our friendship—the way we used to before…"

"It can be different," I suggest optimistically. "We're grown-ups now."

"And you have babies," she adds with an eager grin.

"How about you?" I query curiously. She and Beacon have been together for years.

"Soon. We're working on that. Why don't you come with me to change this little one? I'm saving you from the party."

"There's a party?"

"Or a big reunion... It's hard to tell." Her eyes twinkle mischievously.

Kingston

The backyard is full.

I'm slightly surprised, but what really makes me stop in my tracks is looking at my father tending the grill of what appears to be the outdoor kitchen.

"He helped with the house." Finn stands right beside me.

"Who?"

"Donovan," he answers. "You're staring at him like he's an extraterrestrial and not your dad. I'm guessing he wasn't like this before..."

"No, he wasn't," I confirm. "Have you two reconciled?"

"There's nothing to reconcile," he says. "I didn't have a quarrel with him. He's just a stranger." He leans closer and whispers, "And my father is way better than him—in case you wanna borrow him."

I can't help but chuckle. When he went missing, a nice man, Charles Gil, found him and helped him. The man gave him a new name, a family, and the love he needed to recover. I met him a couple of times and he's a very nice person. But I wouldn't change my dad for… I stop the thought, because it wasn't my brother's choice to switch fathers or to get a new life.

He was dealt a bad hand and thankfully he found a good man who tried his best to give him what he needed at the time.

"What did I say wrong?"

I shake my head and smile. "Nothing. I'm just glad that even when you have another life and you barely remember us, you still let us be a part of yours."

"It's strange to have two families, but I'm grateful," he says and glances at our father. "You're going to be okay, but if you're like him. I think you'll be a good dad."

I frown. "How do you know?"

"I have amnesia, but there are things my heart remembers." He squeezes my shoulder. "Go, say hi to your dad, and stop second-guessing yourself."

Chapter Thirty-Seven

Myka

"I SPOKE TO MOM," Kingston says, his voice thick with emotion. "She's at a retreat, but she hopes to visit us in a few weeks."

I peer at the baby monitor for the tenth time in the past minute, barely able to contain my anxiety. The babies are okay. Piper and Finn are with them. Still... I feel like I should be there, next to them.

"Are you okay with that?" I ask.

"They're fine. We're down here to grab some food, and then

we'll go back upstairs with them, okay?" He presses a gentle kiss to my forehead before grabbing two plates.

I narrow my eyes. "You didn't answer my question."

He sighs. "Yes. I think it's best if she comes later when there aren't so many visitors. Mom and Dad can get too…"

He frowns.

"Are you okay?" I ask again before realizing his dad is right in front of us, holding a plate with different meats.

"Right from the grill," he says, presenting me with a pair of tongs. "What would you like? Your dad brought chorizo—your favorite."

"Thank you," I say, asking for both a piece of chorizo and a steak, grilled medium rare.

"And for you, King?"

Kingston swallows hard and says, "Finn told me you helped with the house."

"It was nothing," Donovan insists, waving away Kingston's gratitude. "I just wanted to make sure everything was ready before you brought the boys home. They're cute." His voice cracks on the last word, and he turns away while adding, "I hope you don't mind if I come down to San Diego to visit them often—same as I do with my other grandchildren."

"You're always welcome here," I offer softly.

Kingston nods, eyes glimmering with tears. "It'll be good to see you often."

"Let me get back to my grill. Finn chose a great one," Donovan says before leaving.

"He's really changing," King mumbles when his father leaves.

"That's good, isn't it?"

He presses a kiss on my cheek and nods, although there's something distant and wistful in his expression. We make our way to the main bedroom, where a small table is set up on the terrace with wine and glasses laid out neatly.

"You made a lot of changes to my room," I observe as we enter, taking in the big bed with luxury bedding and cozy furniture.

Kingston shrugs before leading me to a chair. "I wanted to make sure it was comfortable for the two of us." He pulls my chair so I can sit down.

"You think I'm going to invite you in here?"

"A man can only hope." He pulls my chair so I can sit down.

Gazing out across the horizon, I take in the picture of perfection: the endless ocean, a blazing sun setting against a blue sky, and both of our families together enjoying this special moment—celebrating the start of ours in an unusual way, when usually people do things the other way round—the wedding first, then everything else that follows afterward.

"How do you imagine your life five years from now?" I whisper, my gaze still fixed on the horizon.

"That's a strange question." His voice is filled with curiosity.

"Well, I recall you mentioning that you weren't planning on having children, and you have two." I turn to look at him. "And they're a lifetime commitment."

He gives me a look that I can't decipher and says, "Anywhere in the world with you, our boys, and if possible, another kid or two," he says softly.

"I like the way you think, St. James."

"Good," he says, before he places the plates on the table and takes my hands. King looks into my eyes, and his gaze is filled with an intensity that takes my breath away.

"Your beauty is like the sun, lighting up my world and making everything brighter," he says, his voice soft and poetic. "Your touch is like a warm breeze on a summer's day, soothing my soul and calming my fears. And your love is like the stars in the night sky, guiding me home and giving me hope."

He brushes a strand of hair from my face, his touch sending shivers down my spine. "I want to spend every moment of my life making you feel alive, my love. With you by my side, anything is possible. You are my everything."

I feel tears prickling at the corners of my eyes as I realize how deeply he feels for me. I lean in, pressing my lips to his in a passionate kiss that speaks volumes of the love between us. As we break apart, I rest my forehead against his, feeling his warm breath caress my face.

"All I want is to spend the rest of my life with you, loving you and our children. Would you do me the honor of becoming my wife?"

"Yes. I love you, King," I whisper, my voice filled with emotion.

"I love you more than anything, Myk," he replies, his voice a gentle murmur. "Always."

Epilogue

Kingston

ONE YEAR LATER...

"I got accepted," I hear Shiloh's voice squeaking from the other side of the line.

It's been a year since Lance and Ezra were born. She moved to Seattle, where she's been thriving. We go to visit her often—and the rest of the family. They come down to San Diego during holidays and to celebrate the boys' milestones. We haven't decided yet if we're making this our permanent residence or if we'll be going back to Seattle. All that matters to us is that the boys are happy.

My relationship with Dad has improved a lot. We're still a work in progress. Mom is also making some changes in her life. I guess it's a way to ensure that none of her children shuts her out of theirs.

"She got into Columbia, King," Myk calls out.

"But I'm still looking at my options," I hear Shiloh say. "Are you sure it doesn't matter where I choose to go?"

"It doesn't matter," I confirm, and I perk up when I hear a sound from the baby monitor. When I glance at the screen, I spot Lance stretching and Ezra already sitting.

"Time's up," I say, tapping the desk. "The boys are up and ready to destroy the house."

"Give a kiss to them from me."

"Of course, we will," Myk says. "Call me later today, if not Sunday as usual."

"Probably Sunday. I have to study for tomorrow," I hear Shiloh say before the call disconnects.

"Stay here," I say, kissing her lips and then her bump.

"I'm pregnant, not sick," she reminds me.

"And have I mentioned you look gorgeous carrying our baby?"

We're having a baby girl in less than two months. The three little ones will be close in age, we believe that will help forge a close bond. We don't have a name yet, but it'll come to us when we meet her.

When I arrive at the boys' room, they look at me with adoration and say in unison, "Daddy!"

Them saying that word is everything in my life. It is just as perfect as when Myk says, *I love you.*

"You know what we should do next summer?" Myk asks, picking up Lance.

"Go on vacation?"

"I was thinking of organizing a wedding," she says. "The small reunion after having your cousin marry us was good, but a big party with our little ones…"

"Anything for you," I say, taking her into my arms. Kissing her fiercely.

Sometimes, Myka jokes that we accidentally fell in love, but she's wrong. This was meant to be. Before her, my heart had been closed off for anyone. I guarded it fiercely, keeping it locked away from the world, afraid of what might happen if I exposed myself to vulnerability.

But then, she came along. The most wonderful woman in the world. She's different from anyone I know. She made me ache to taste her, to learn every detail of her being.

In the beginning, she may have set rules in place, and I broke them—accidentally on purpose. But nothing between us was accidental. Our hearts and souls fell in love before our minds accepted the inevitable. We are a perfectly imperfect match and… it all started with a WildMatch.

Now we have forever to write and rewrite the rules for our love, our life, our future—together.

DYING for more Kingston and Mika?

Go here for another exclusive extended epilogue!

https://www.subscribepage.com/accidentallyinlove

Want to read Teddy's story?

Read it here >>> https://claudiayburgoa.com/wp/after-the-vows/

Or are you curious about Finnegan's life?

Read it here >>> https://claudiayburgoa.com/wp/the-end-of-me/

Dear Reader

Thank you so much for reading ACCIDENTALLY IN LOVE.

I hope you enjoyed it as much as I did writing it. I'll be honest with you, Mika Cantú and Kingston St. James were a very unexpected couple, but they're the perfect match. A few of my alpha readers and plot consultants told me they weren't meant to be but… as you can see they're meant for each other.

Our next St. James brother is Myles. I can't wait to see what our favorite journalist has in store.

If you loved this story as much as I did, I would love if you could leave a review on Bookbub or your favorite retailer.

Sending all my love,
Claudia xoxo

Excerpt

I hope you enjoyed Accidentally in Love keep reading for an extended excerpt of:

Until Next Time (Zach & Autumn)

Wrong Text, Right Love (Persy & Ford)

Didn't Expect You (Nyx & Nate)

Wrong Text, Right Love

Saturday, April 4th

"I thought you were like the Beast, but you're Peter Pan without the green leggings," Martha yells, shoving my pants against my torso.

Ok, the Peter Pan reference I get, but who the fuck is the Beast?

"Maybe I'm wrong and you're Rapunzel, waiting for some innocent woman to rescue you from your Ivory tower," she continues her rant, and I think I get it now. She's trying to compare me to Disney princes—and even princesses. "Enough is enough. I'm done loving you. I tried and I tried, but you never gave anything back."

Whoa, we're throwing the *L* word?

Her next-door neighbor has the door open and is watching the show. I know what this looks like, and I'm pretty sure she's thinking: The guy being thrown out of the house wearing boxer briefs with 'I just fucked' hair means he cheated. Not only that, she caught him.

Or, there's a second possibility. He doesn't want to take the next step.

Nosy neighbor nods and scrunches her nose, as she confirms her suspicions. *This asshole has been stringing this poor woman along for years.*

I could set things straight and put her mind at ease. There's another side to the story. Martha and I met a few months ago at the grocery store. She was pretty and funny. We exchanged numbers, and after a few texts, we tried to give this friendship a go.

"We agreed this was just for fun," I remind Martha.

"We had *more than fun*," she claims.

For fuck's sake, why did she believe this could be more? It is always the same. I've yet to find a woman who says, "I'm developing feelings for you, and I think we should stop seeing each other." Throwing words like, "we should move in together," in the middle of fucking is not the way to move forward.

Honestly, I just can't seem to do things right. If I don't tell them up front that we are only fuck buddies, I get shit when they want more. If I do, they ignore me—because they think they can be my exception.

A friend of mine says that my issue is due to the way they see me. A lonely, introverted bachelor. Women think they have just the right pussy to save me from my sad life—and change me for the better. First rule about choosing a partner, don't expect people to change for you. You are only attracted

Accidentally in Love

to them and your hormones are wanting more of him —or her.

That doesn't mean you are in love. It means you are passionate about them. You are physically attracted, but if you want the person to adapt to your needs and you won't accept them as they are, that's definitely not love.

Love is extremely complicated and should be handled with care. I choose not to deal with it.

Albert Einstein once said, "You can't blame gravity for falling in love."

I have nothing against relationships. In fact, I had a couple of those during my teens. Love is messy. Relationships are complicated. The logistics to hold onto an emotional partnership is too complex and dreary.

It requires more than dinner, sex, flowers, and chocolates. Both parties have to agree to more than just monogamy. They have to surrender to one another and walk blindly into a place where they only exist with each other. I can't imagine the effort that is required to maintain something like that, and to what end?

Look, it's not like I've been shying away from love. I tried being part of a couple. At fifteen, I dated Wendy Robins. She lived across the street from my home. She was cute. We got to second base, but her family moved when the school year was over. I never heard from her again. At sixteen it was Sandra Boyt, one of my brother's friends. We had a good time, until I refused to go to prom, and she dumped me for some other dude —I can't even remember his name.

At this point in my life, I'm practical. When I go out with a woman, I tell her right away, *This is just sex. I'm not looking for anything permanent.*

The whole concept of forever works for a lot of people—until they break up or divorce.

Forever is not for me.

It has nothing to do with some *Little Prince syndrome*—that's the technical term for the condition. The *Peter Pan syndrome* sounds too cliché—and let's be clear, it's not a mental illness.

Why did I adopt this philosophy?

It's a combination between my parents' messy divorce, the fact that I've never been in love, and that once upon a time I was named the future of technology. People who I never met flocked around me. It wasn't easy to tell apart friends from a foe. My circle of trust became microscopic.

My twin brother insists I'm like this because when we were born, I got the brains and he got the heart.

Maybe he's right. It's fucking unbelievable that I've never been in love.

Never.

Is there such a thing as falling in love and I'm immune to it? I'm living proof that it is real.

The other day, I was at the dentist's office, and the receptionist was listening to some 'dating expert' on talk radio—or maybe it was her computer. It really doesn't matter. The point is that this woman was discussing the subject of falling in love with her partner—again. I was pretty confused at first, until she explained further about a so-called *love cycle*.

According to this 'authority in love,' a couple has to keep the flame burning for each other. Tend to their relationship the same way farmers do with their lands. Each season is different. They plant, they water, they harvest, they clean, so next season, they can start all over again. When a caller asked her what falling in love meant, her answer made me laugh.

According to this 'expert,' falling is different from being in love, and it all starts with a feeling that makes someone want to be next to *the* person. Falling is embracing the out of control, overwhelming emotion that accelerates one's heart into the speed of light. One knows that they're in love when they make a special place in their life for that other person.

Living in love (yes, that's how she phrased it) is different, though. It means that someone stays willingly with their significant other despite their flaws and even when they drive you crazy.

If you are in love, you want to stick around the other person, even when you don't like them at times.

I wanted to tell her, *Lady, your advice is shit. If someone doesn't like the person they are with, they should move on.*

Why would I choose to be around someone who I can't stand when it's clear we are not compatible?

It's obvious that woman is from another planet or hasn't met me. My guess is that she got some fancy degree in shit-talk that allows her to spew crap. She only knows a few people. There are billions of humans in this world, and we don't all fall in love or even need it to live.

According to that woman—and maybe all the women I've been with—I'm shallow because I can't see past appearances. It's not about accepting flaws or loving what's inside. This world is complicated enough to also be forced to stay around people who don't make one's life better.

I just do what I love the most. Sex.

Sex is the only reason why I bother finding fuck buddies. Let me tell you, I deliver a fan-fucking-tastic time. But that's exactly where my problem begins. I was taught to be thoughtful and caring about what's entrusted to me.

Women trust me with their bodies, and I do my best to treat them like queens. But it never fails. They always want more. It doesn't matter that we both agreed it'd be casual. They demand more from me. Then, they urge me to reciprocate their feelings. I'm physically and emotionally incapable of following through with what they want from me.

In my opinion, love exists. It's just not for everyone.

Most of all, it's not for me.

Let's be logical. Not everything in this world is for everyone. We are all different. I am the kind of guy who doesn't fall in love. I'm not heartless. Just because I don't wear my heart on my sleeve, it doesn't mean that I don't have one. I'm wired differently.

Some men struggle to describe what love is. Me? I can't even feel it. Which brings me to this exact moment when the woman I've been fucking for the last couple of months makes the unilateral decision to modify our agreement—and if I don't comply, it's over.

"I thought we had a connection," she repeats. "I've never felt this way before."

Can we pause for a second?

What Martha infers is that I'm the first lover she's had who isn't a selfish bastard. I'll let you in on a little secret. Sex is more enjoyable when you put your partner's pleasure before your own. Personally, it turns me on to know that the woman I am with is high on endorphins *because of me.*

Now, fast forward to this moment. I can tell her one of two things: "You should be careful about who you invite into your bed," or "I was upfront with you when I said this won't be more than sex."

There's no use in discussing this any further. It's over.

I put on my pants and walk toward the staircase. I slip on my sneakers before climbing down the stairs.

Why do people complicate everything?

Life is simple.

Relationships should be easy, not some crazy affair where you have to play a part. Perhaps that's why I don't fit well with anyone. Sometimes, not even my family.

One thing I can guarantee, I'll never apologize for being myself.

Women expect romance. Most of them define romance as all those clichés that happen in chick flicks. Guy running through an airport to ask for forgiveness because he is a dumb-ass. Or through the streets of Manhattan. Let's say I follow the entire narrative of romance and make a woman fall in love with me. I mean really fall in love, not just the 'high on endorphins, please give me another dose because I can't live without an orgasm' kind of feeling.

What happens next?

I can't guarantee that I'll be in love too. And If I do fall, what am I supposed to do with it?

Hypothetically speaking, I let my guard down, give away my secrets and my entire life to one person. Nothing guarantees that the person I trusted will not come back to destroy me.

Again, I'm not speaking from experience. Unless my mother counts. She left my father when I was five. However, I've witnessed many divorces and broken relationships to know what I'm talking about. I've watched people falling apart, helplessly, as their worlds come crashing down.

In all fairness, I accept that not every relationship ends up in catastrophe. There's my father's second marriage. He found a good woman who makes him happy—more like they make each other happy. My stepbrother and his wife are yet another couple who seem to be content. I don't like them, but they've been together for ten years.

That's when the theory about soulmates comes into play. Because these couples make it through *everything*.

Maybe the idea that there's one person who imprinted with another before the beginning of time is real. Or, perhaps, it's some false ideal we want to grab onto so Hallmark can sell more Valentine's cards during the month of February.

Either way, I'm not sure how this heart-soulmate-love business works, or if it's even real. Honestly, I don't care to find out. The closest I ever got to that moment when a person sees someone and feels like they were punched in the stomach and can barely recover was when I was still living at home.

There was this girl I used to see around the neighborhood during the holidays. Perfect smile, always wearing colorful clothing. She had a whole happy thing going on for her. Every year, I'd see her around and get that sweaty-hands-heart-pounding feeling. I never knew where she lived. Getting closer would've been kind of creepy because she was young or maybe too short.

Who knows?

I never met her, and yet, sometimes, I still think about her smile.

It was contagious.

When you saw her, you just smiled with her.

No one has ever made me smile the way she did. Maybe that's why I can't open myself to anyone or settle for anything but the best. That feeling that closed up my throat when I saw her… I've never felt it again.

Continue Reading Wrong Text, Right Love

Didn't Expect You

Nyx

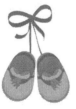

All my adult life I've been fighting to be somewhat normal. To be the most conventional one in the family—or the only one for that matter.

My parents are...different. My three siblings... Well, they aren't like our parents, but they stand out easily in any crowd.

Not me. Or at least I try to stay away from people's radars, unlike them.

While we were growing up, my parents believed we could learn more from the world than in a classroom. Were they right?

The jury is still out deliberating.

One thing I can say is that my dad is one of the wisest, most clueless men in the world. I understand how ambiguous that sounds, but my father isn't like any conventional sixty-three-year-old guy. Octavio Brassard is unique among any men. He lives by his own rules and has a license to teach young adults about ancient civilizations.

According to Dad, we're here to learn how to love, how to live, and how to preserve this world. Not that we, the human race, are doing a great job at any of those things. He insists that the most important moments in our life happen unexpectedly. That's why we have to stop and smell the roses. Maybe one of those special moments is the one that transforms our lives.

In that split second, we could find our destiny.

He's a philosopher, a poet, and one of the most loving people I know. He pushes us, his children and students, to believe in ourselves and always pursue our dreams. Take life by the balls. And no, my father doesn't believe in censoring our language.

Something else I learned from my parents is that family comes before anything and everyone.

This is why I'm spending my weekend working with my oldest brother, Eros, who like my father, is a dreamer. He doesn't like to think much about the bottom line, rather what he can do to change the world.

"I could be with Persy drinking margaritas," I protest, as I go through the partnership proposal he received from LNC Investments.

I could spend my time with my sister, who I haven't seen that much during the past couple of months.

"Persy is actually drinking some strawberry lager Dad made," he corrects me. "It tastes like fruity shit."

I glare at him. "I like fruity shit."

"Fruity doesn't mean refined," he informs me. "You two need to learn to drink better brands and less sugar."

Sighing, I finish reading the contract. We're never going to agree on the subject. He thinks spending a thousand dollars on a bottle of single malt is better than drinking margaritas. We'll have to agree to disagree.

"Listen, you shouldn't be signing this," I suggest. "Persy and I will amend her book deal and—"

"It's going to take me years to recover her investment," he interrupts me. "These guys don't need the money right away. She does."

He is right. Our sister lent him her savings. The amount included the advance she received from Blackstone and Morgan Press, the publishing company that bought the rights to her next book. A book she doesn't want to write because it's off-brand and forcing her to divulge more about her life on social media than she usually does. I'm trying to fix her current contract so she can change the title and the subject. But if we can't come to an agreement, she'll have to give the money back so I can terminate the contract.

I sigh.

"Thirty-five percent is a lot," I say, changing the argument as I continue reading through the partnership proposal. "We need to negotiate the terms before you sign anything. I understand that they are practically financing the entire operation, but…"

I pull out a calculator and run some numbers. "You're not earning any money for at least five years. Where are you supposed to live and what are you going to eat?"

"Funny that you mention this," he says, giving me his boyish grin. "You have an extra room in your house."

"No!" I answer with determination.

I have two guest rooms. I love my siblings, but I can only stand living with them for so long. Just earlier this year, Persy stayed with me for almost six months and even when we had fun, we both concur that we needed our own place. We're too old to have roommates. I can't imagine what it'd be like to live with Eros for five years—or until he gets his shit together. I'm going to become his maid, parent, and… No, thank you.

"Nyx, at least let me explain my plan to you." His pleading voice doesn't change my mind. In fact, I cross my arms. "I sell my place—"

"You have two mortgages on that house. You owe more than you'll get for it. You have to be sensible about your finances," I remind him, shaking my head. "Why do I always have to sound like the oldest one in this family?"

He shrugs. "You always liked to boss me around while we

were growing up. Show that you were responsible. It's your thing. Just like Persy likes to analyze people. I watch over you three."

He's right. That's been our dynamic since we were kids. It might have to do with the way we were raised. Our baby sister, Calliope, doesn't fit in this dynamic, and maybe that's why she doesn't like us so much.

"No, we're going to go back to these Chadwick brothers and we're going to cut you a deal that will be beneficial for everyone," I state. "Do we have an understanding?"

He salutes me. "You're the boss."

There's this idea that the person we become is partly defined by the order in which we come into our family. It's part of the sibling hierarchy. The oldest becomes the teacher to the rest of the siblings. Whoever established that theory didn't know the Brassard siblings. We are four, one brother and three sisters. Eros is the oldest. I'm the second out of four. Then comes my sister, Persy, and Calliope is the baby.

In theory, Eros should be our teacher. The one who takes care of us. Most days I'm the one who is rescuing everyone and saving them from not fucking up their lives. Maybe it has to do with my parents' philosophy. They believe that making mistakes is what forges our character. I keep telling them that there are mistakes, and then there are times when people should avoid failing. Letting others commit errors so you can learn isn't always smart. What if it's something that can bankrupt us, get us thrown in jail, or kill us?

Earlier today it was my brother. Thankfully, I was able to change the original partnership he was about to sign, and he got to save his home.

More like, I won't be having him as a roommate, and we won't end up killing each other because he's a slob.

Now, I'm on my way to talk some sense into Calliope. Most days I'm thankful for Persy. She's not only the most down to earth of my siblings, but she's also my best friend. Maybe the whole theory about birth order has some truth to it. She's only ten months younger than me. We have a connection like not many do. We understand each other, and sometimes we even guess how the other one is feeling.

As I'm about to ring the doorbell to the apartment complex where Callie lives, there's a person coming out who lets me in and even smiles. I blink a couple of times and shrug. What happened to security? I climb the stairs to the fourth story and knock on the door.

A male voice answers, "In a minute."

Not sure if the guy understands how long a minute is because only two seconds later the door opens. It's a tallish guy. By tallish I mean under six feet, lanky, and in a dire need of a trim. No, I don't have anything against guys who have long hair. There are some that look hotter with a mane. This guy though, he needs…a shower, a brush, and clean clothes.

"We didn't order take out," he says.

"I'm here to see Calliope, my sister," I inform him.

"Cal?" he asks and studies me. "You kind of look like her, but uptight."

"Is she here?"

"No, she moved out a week ago," he states.

"Who are you?"

"Ron," he answers. "I'm subleasing this place."

Subleasing the place? I'm blown away by those three words. She's not allowed to do that. Did he even sign a contract? Because I don't remember signing one where I agreed to let this man live in this apartment. I take a deep breath and ask calmly, "Did she leave you a forwarding address?"

He shakes his head. "No. You should talk to your sister, not me."

I hate to agree with him, but there's nothing I can say to him that'll make this right. Other than kicking him out of the place because technically he is living here without my consent.

"Thank you, I appreciate your time," I say and leave.

On my way to the car, I dial Callie's number. She sends me to voicemail, so I try again, again, and again until she finally answers, "What do you want?"

"Where are you?"

"Far away from you," she states.

Why do you always have to answer like a petulant fifteen-year-old? I want to protest, but I don't. Instead, I say, "I take it you made the decision to move out of the state. Did it occur to you to tell us about it?"

"As I said the last time we spoke, I'm done with your meddling," she comments. "In fact, I'm done with you. Lose my number."

"Well then, when will you be sending me the money I loaned you to buy your car and the deposit to rent the apartment where this Ron character lives?" I question. "Furthermore, this apartment is under my name too, and I didn't sign any agreement to sublease the place to him. My name is on that leasing contract."

"If I were Persy, you would've helped me move. Instead, you're demanding money that I don't have," she argues. "It's a verbal contract which should be binding. He is good for it. Don't worry about what can happen to your precious name."

I sigh. "That argument is so old it doesn't have the same effect. Calliope, our parents are going to be heartbroken and worried if you don't tell them where you are. At least give them a courtesy call."

"They are the reason I'm running away from this family. Have you realized that they aren't normal? They embarrass us. While growing up, I could never bring friends to the house because I never knew what they would do," she explains. "Please, don't tell me you aren't ashamed of them. How many times have you brought a boyfriend to the house? None, because you know it's horrifying to introduce them to Octavio and Edna Brassard. And then, there's Persephone. *She's a famous sexologist.*"

Our parents are unique. Yes, they can be a handful and we have to control their narrative sometimes. However, I'll take those two above many other parents who are abusive, neglectful, or plain. Persy is an influencer, a therapist, and yes, she markets herself as a sexologist. There's nothing wrong with her career. I'd be concerned if she was a criminal.

"We never had normal," she continues, and I laugh. "Stop laughing at me!"

I clear my throat and say, "I laugh because you're not making sense. You sound like a petulant child having a tantrum because you're not getting your way."

"You never take me seriously, Nyx. You think you are the smartest one of us. Just because you have a fancy office, a nice house, and a luxury car, you think that you are better than us. You are not!"

"Callie, stop while you're ahead," I warn her.

"You're upset because I'm telling you the truth. And the truth always hurts. You're pathetic, Nyx. Your life is fucking sad. Just boring and plain like you."

She's not wrong about being boring or having a life. I'm nothing like Persy or her. One thing I hate about my baby sister is that when she strikes, she hits where it hurts the most.

"Listen, Callie, we love you even when you're rude to us because you are our little sister. I stopped liking you a long time ago. You became this entitled woman that I can't stand, and you know what...I'm done being the one trying to keep this family together," I say. "Not only that, I'm done with you. If you want to play martyr and tell the world that you escaped your crazy family, that's up to you. Just don't come back groveling for money."

I hang up and fire up a text to Persy.

Nyx: *What are you up to?*

Persy: *I'm hanging out with Ford. Need me?*

Nyx: *No, I wanted to gossip about your hot grumpy neighbor. I guess we'll have to do it another time.*

Persy: *Liar. What's happening?*

I smile because she knows me too well.

Nyx: *Nothing important, I swear. Talk to you soon.*

Persy: *Love you, Nyx.*

Nyx: *Love you, Pers.*

As much as I would love to tell her what is happening with Callie, I don't do it. One of these days, I'll give her the Spark Notes. I just wish I had someone in my life who was there for me when I feel like the weight on my shoulders is too heavy to carry. Maybe I just have to dump it in some abandoned alley and be done with everyone.

I drive back to my house where I place my leftovers in the refrigerator and put on my pajamas. Instead of turning on the television to find some numbing tv show to watch, I pull out my tablet from my messenger bag and start working on my next case.

Callie isn't wrong. I don't have a life. Boring... I don't think I'm boring. I just don't have time to let my hair loose and just live for pleasure. I should add that to my to-do list. Maybe at the bottom of it. One day I'll get to it.

Continue Reading Didn't Expect You

Until Next Time

Zach

You see that guy wearing a dark suit, crisp dress shirt, and a tie? Yes, the guy with dark brown hair and blue eyes. Wait, you're looking at my twin brother. I mean the one next to him. The man with the vacant expression. The poor asshole who can barely stand and would like to be anywhere but in this cemetery.

This isn't the best time to meet me. I'm not at my best.

Under different circumstances, I'm the one who'd be making you feel welcome during this gathering—even when it's a funeral. I could give you an insight into Zachary David St. James. My friends call me Zach. I'm twenty-seven, and the owner of Café Fusion. If you're ever in Boston, come and check it out. As you can see, I'm down on my luck. My wife of six months died in an accident last Monday.

I believe in love.

The kind of love that wraps your heart to your soul and hand delivers it to the person you're meant to be with. I'm not saying I've been planning my wedding since I was six. That'd be my baby sister. I just knew that one day I'd get married and start a family.

When I met Calliope Brassard, I thought, this is it—she is love personified.

Callie was supposed to be the one I'd spend the rest of my life with. She was supposed to be my eternity—if that's even a term.

I chuckle inside my head. If Callie heard me call her love personified or my eternity, she'd be laughing at me. She used to say I was corny. Too corny. At the beginning of our relationship, I thought we were complete opposites who fit perfectly. In the end...

I stare at the mahogany casket that's being lowered into the ground. This trip isn't what I thought when Calliope said she wanted to take a trip to celebrate our six-month anniversary this weekend. She hoped we'd go to a luxury beach, like Plage des Sablettes in France. I suggested we travel to Seattle, maybe spend the weekend in Silver Lake with my family. It's the fifth anniversary since we lost my brother, Archer. She was uncomfortable with the idea of going to his celebration of life.

And here we are, at Holyhood Cemetery—ironically, celebrating her life.

Burke, my twin brother, squeezes my shoulder as the priest sprinkles holy water. The next step is to toss a red rose that lands on the mahogany casket. Callie preferred orchids, but my sister, Teddy, said that roses are more practical. After releasing the red flower that falls slowly on top of the elegant box, I look around. My three brothers and my baby sister follow my lead.

They welcomed Callie as part of the St. James family, even when they thought our wedding was too sudden.

Was it sudden?

At least I got to be with her for six months before…I can't even think about her being dead. A part of me is waiting for her to walk up and say, "What did I miss?"

"Why her?" I hear a woman cry. When I look up, I spot Callie's mom sobbing.

I don't know why it happened to Callie, and I don't plan on asking. If I begin to ask questions, I'll drive myself crazy. Whatifs are also forbidden because I can't deal with the answers.

"It's time for us to go," Burke says, placing his hand on my shoulder and directing me to where I have to walk.

My twin and Teddy have been taking care of everything, including me. I've been a zombie ever since two police officers arrived at the coffee shop Monday evening to tell me that my wife wasn't picking up her phone because she was dead. I was hoping it was a tantrum because I didn't want to go to France. No. Callie was dead.

"Are you sure those are Callie's parents?" I hear Teddy ask.

"Yes." Burke sounds annoyed. "Why do you ask?"

"I remember *her* saying they were horrible people. Look at her sisters. They are crying for her. I—"

"Stop," I order Teddy. "We're not discussing Callie."

She nods, giving me an apologetic look.

I know what she's about to say, and I'm not ready to listen to any of it. I just lost my wife.

I glance one last time to where I left her to rest, alone. If there's something Callie feared, it was being by herself. I feel like I should stay behind with her. That's what they used to do in Egypt, wasn't it? I lift my gaze, looking at her parents, who are archeologists. They'd know, but I guess it's too late to ask them if what I'm doing is right. One thing is for sure: I don't care to uncover any secrets or learn more about my wife. All I know is that I'll never listen to her voice or see her bright smile again.

All I know is that I probably died with her.

>>>> Continue Reading Something Like Love

Claudia is an award winning, USA Today bestselling author.

She writes alluring, thrilling stories about complicated women and the men who take their breaths away. She lives in Denver, Colorado with her husband and her youngest two children. She has a sweet Bichon, Macey, who thinks she's the ruler of the house—she's only partially right. Hanna, the cuddliest and cutest Havanese/Maltese, is the one who rules them all.

When Claudia is not writing, you can find her reading, knitting, or just hanging out with her family. At nights, she likes to binge watch shows with his equally geeky husband.

To find more about Claudia:
  website
  Sign up for her newsletter: Newsletter

Also By Claudia Burgoa

Be sure to sign up for my newsletter where you'll receive news about upcoming releases, sneak previous, and also FREE books from other bestselling authors.

ACCIDENTALLY IN LOVE is also available in Audio

The Baker's Creek Billionaire Brothers Series

Loved You Once

A Moment Like You

Defying Our Forever

Call You Mine

As We Are

Yours to Keep

Paradise Bay Billionaire Brothers

My Favorite Night

Faking The Game

Can't Help Love

Along Came You

My Favorite Mistake

The Way of Us

Meant For Me

Finally Found You

Where We Belong

Heartwood Lake Secret Billionaires

A Place Like You

Dirty Secret Love

Love Unlike Ours

Through It All

Better than Revenge

Fade into us

An Unlikely Story

Hard to love

Against All Odds Series

Wrong Text, Right Love

Didn't Expect You

Love Like Her

Until Next Time, Love

Something Like Love

Accidentally in Love

Forget About Love

Waiting for Love

Decker Family Novels

Unexpected Everlasting:

Suddenly Broken

Suddenly Us

Somehow Everlasting:

Almost Strangers

Strangers in Love

Perfect Everlasting:

Who We Are

Who We Love

Us After You

Covert Affair Duet:

After The Vows

Love After Us

The Downfall of Us:

The End of Me

When Forever Finds Us

Requiem for Love:

Reminders of Her

The Symphony of Us

Impossibly Possible:

The Lies About Forever

The Truth About Love

Second Chance Sinners :

Pieces of Us

Somehow Finding Us

The Spearman Brothers

Maybe Later

Then He Happened

Once Upon a Holiday

Almost Perfect

Luna Harbor

Finally You

Perfectly You

Always You

Truly You

My One

My One Regret

My One Desire

The Everhart Brothers

Fall for Me

Fight for Me

Perfect for Me

Forever with Me

Mile High Billionaires

Finding My Reason

Something Like Hate

Someday, Somehow

Standalones

Chasing Fireflies

Until I Fall

Christmas in Kentbury

Chaotic Love Duet

Begin with You

Back to You

Co-writing

Holiday with You

Home with You

Here with You

All my books are interconnected standalone, except for the duets, but if you want a reading order, I have it here ↪ Reading Order

Manufactured by Amazon.ca
Bolton, ON

34282473R00166